Tango Sho'...

- cafe Tortoni -
- book store /cafe — del Tango 825
- 1day trip to Ungue
- La Boce (bario) taxi - green
  go 4pm

Clothes: brasie style La Martine

Happy Tango

SALLYCAT'S GUIDE TO DANCING IN BUENOS AIRES

2ND EDITION

- Carlos di Salli
- Alfredo de Angeli
- Francisco Canaro
- Juan D'Ariento

Sally Blake

PIROTTA PRESS LTD

First published in 2010 by

Pirotta Press Ltd
PO Box 1154
Warrington
WA4 9LD
United Kingdom

This second edition published 2012

pirottapress.com
sallycatway.com/happytango

ISBN 978-0-9565306-1-5

Cover photography by Julie-Anne Cosgrove
julieannecosgrove.com
First edition cover design by SoroDesign
sorodesign.com
with second edition amendments by SallyBlakeDesigns
sallyblakedesigns.co.uk

Disclaimer
Every effort was made to ensure that the information contained in this
book was correct at the time of going to press. Because locations, times
of operations and neighbourhood circumstances may change, the
author and the publisher do not assume and hereby disclaim any
liability to any party for any loss, damage or inconvenience arising from
inaccuracies, omissions or the use of this guide.

The month after I published the first edition of
Happy Tango, my beloved Mum was diagnosed with
oral cancer, though she had never smoked. She died
on 19 July 2011, aged seventy-four. I dedicate this
second edition of the book to her, Judy Townsend.
I miss you Mum, but you are with me in everything I do.

Without the love and support of my Mum and Dad,
and my sisters Jane and Jo, I would never have
found the courage to journey to Argentina.
Without Carlos, who walks with patience beside me
every day, my heart would never have spilled over with
the love required to write **Happy Tango**.
You precious souls, I thank you.

THE REVIEWS

Since its publication in 2010, *Happy Tango* has received more than 30 'five star' reviews on Amazon, plus many enthusiastic responses by email, via Facebook message and in person. Here's a sample of what people have written.

"***Happy Tango*** is completely spot-on! This book should be handed out at Ezeiza airport to all those with tango shoes in their suitcase... Sally's '11 Rules' for dancing in BsAs and the '20 Places to Try First' are simply brilliant..."

"After just returning from my eighteenth trip to Buenos Aires, I can say that Sally's book passes my credibility test with flying colors — her accuracy in describing parts of the scene I know about gives me great confidence in relying on her information about parts that are unfamiliar to me."

"Great!!!! If you only take one book with you, this should be the one."

"If you're going to Buenos Aires, you need this book. Read it before you go; wear out its pages while you are there. Sally has done an excellent job of taking just enough of the mystery out of what can be an intimidating scene... If you dance Argentine tango, you will love this book."

"No stone has been left unturned regarding the 'must knows' of tango in BA... Even after much research since my last trip, nothing measures up to this book."

"Essential!! Applicable to tango dancers worldwide AND is a MUST BUY if you plan to dance in BsAs!"

"... a very easy, extremely informative read and the advice given is absolutely brilliant."

"This is an absolute 'must' companion for you while embarking on your tango adventures in Buenos Aires... I know that I have discovered things that would have otherwise taken me months to find."

"I could have saved hours trawling through tango blogs trying to gather information if I had had this little book."

"Priceless advice at a reasonable price"

"... clearly the best available introduction to the Buenos Aires tango world — and it's equally useful for us domestic tangueros and tangueras. Sally's insights are based on her practical experience among dancers, and she delivers her message with wit and verve... Do not visit a milonga again till you've read and absorbed her book!"

"*Happy Tango* provides readers with the inside scoop on the Buenos Aires tango scene and is an absolute 'must read' for any visitor — first timer or repeat traveller. I can attest that Sally's tips are absolutely bang on and will help the reader really get the most out of their Buenos Aires tango experience."

"A 'must read' whether you are going to dance in Buenos Aires or not!"

"I feel like I'm traveling with a friend... This is a book that will go in my carry-on and be re-read on the plane ride."

"Covers everything you need to know in one concise text, undiluted by irrelevant information that you may find in general guides, and at the same time acknowledges the emotional aspects of this tango so close to the heart."

"The level of specificity and detail in the book cannot be stated enough. I feel like I have been given a complete dossier on Buenos Aires and the Argentine tango scene..."

"Sally encourages you to find the venues where you feel most comfortable, to find your 'tango home', and this helped me a lot in deciding where to go in the evening... packed with useful tips... an indispensable tango dance guidebook for Buenos Aires."

"... a great read for every tango dancer — even if you are only dreaming of heading off to dance in Buenos Aires..."

"If you're going to Buenos Aires to dance tango you should make *Happy Tango* your bible. It's a one-stop shop for everything you need — and that's what I'll be telling all the tango dancers I know!"

"She understands the tango scene, and the problems foreign tourists can face, more than most — in fact, probably more than anyone."

"Excellent book — totally accurate and helpful... Well worth the money."

"This book will turn a good tango holiday into the trip of a lifetime. Don't leave for Buenos Aires without it!"
Steve Morrall, *Tango UK* **(TangoUK.co.uk)**

"A well-written, sane, straightforward book about tango in BsAs and elsewhere. I like it, and will recommend it widely to beginners especially. Everybody needs to read the 'Rules'. Great job!"
Andreas Wichter — teacher and DJ at the *Tangokombinat* **(tangokombinat.de)**

"... a very well-written, clear and sensible guide to the experience of dancing tango in Buenos Aires and Sally's tone is rational and no-nonsense... I would VERY highly recommend this book to anyone who is visiting Buenos Aires for the first time."
Terpsichoral Tangoaddict — Buenos Aires based dancer and blogger at *Tango Addiction* **(tangoaddiction.wordpress.com)**

"With lovely stories, self-declared 'Sallycat Spanglish' and disarming honesty, this book is a great read. It is an invaluable tool for those planning a tango holiday and a lovely insight for those who are not."
Carole Edrich (www.dancetog.com) for *Dance Today* **(www.dance-today.co.uk)**

If you enjoy *Happy Tango*, please consider writing a review of the book on Amazon, Facebook, Twitter or anywhere at all. It's great for me to hear that *Happy Tango* is doing its job, and you will help the book to reach more people who may need it. Thank you.

Sallycat

ACKNOWLEDGEMENTS

On **Happy Tango**'s journey from seed of an idea to being, The Universe has sent me many angels.

My editor, the novelist and poet Mike Stocks (**mikestocks.com**), is absolutely the most generous and talented of them all, and I think of him as the book's guardian angel — from 7000 miles away in Edinburgh, Scotland, with loving but brutal honesty and hours and hours of his precious time, he gave me a masterclass in the process of writing a book worth reading. I can never thank him enough.

Julie-Anne Cosgrove (**julieannecosgrove.com**), my sub-editor angel and friend, who with hawk-eyed blue pen in masterful hand, transformed my Sallycat language from flawed silver to gleaming gold, who was unafraid to tell me the truth in her determination to make **Happy Tango** the best it could be, and who did it all out of the kindness of her huge heart. She sub-edited the second edition too, I am delighted to say.

Helen Coyle (**indyeditorial.com**), editorial consultant and fellow adventurer, who arrived in my life in January 2009, when my belief in my ability to write had faltered — her confidence in me set my words flowing afresh, and she has been by my side with unflagging encouragement ever since.

Tony Parkes, who showed me more red ink than my editor himself, in his efforts to ensure an accurate male perspective, and who suggested the inclusion of The (essential) Week at a Glance.

My test readers and research partners-in-crime along the way, from word one, back in September 2008 — Caroline Weynerowski, Yasmin Zaman, Amanda Watson, Bridget Lynch, Rachel Stevenson (whose boundless enthusiasm carried me from the first to the second draft), Catrin Strong, Sally Bibb, Shaun Orpen, Maggie Fawcett, María José Iribarne, Debbi Hobson, Cherie Magnus (author of **The Church of Tango: A Memoir**), Mark Brooker, Nikki Mellor, Matthew Cooper, Gabrielle Stein, Amy Allison, Charlotte Williams, Andrew Emerson, Joanne Emerson, Tom Williams and Tammy Williams.

The *tangueras, tangueros* and a few non-dancers worldwide who made time to answer my questions, help me, send me a gem of information, or who allowed me to quote them — Nina Ofenböck, Kieron Taylor, Ruth Burton, Annabella Chang, Scott Baldwin, Anne Moore, Donna Moore, Tina Ferrari, Holly Foster, Anne Li, Soobin Sunwoo, Anna Ellala, Owen McArdle, Henry Shawdon, Louise Longdin, Zoe Winters, Sandra Bao, Cliff Williamson, Simon Barnes, Mariana Docampo, Santiago Velez, Mary Ann Henderson, Brad Bunnin, Katie Hale, José Padilla, Margareta Westergård (author of **Tango Passion and the Rules of the Game**), my friends Rachel Sloan and Maggie Cowan-Hughes, and anyone and everyone that I have unintentionally missed out.

The Buenos Aires English Speaking Writers' Group who between them, Wednesday after Wednesday, motivated me to keep writing, even when I wanted to chuck it all in the shredder and run off to Antarctica.

The world-famous author Susan Jeffers PhD (**www.susanjeffers.com**) and her inspirational book and trademarked phrase Feel the Fear and Do It Anyway®, used by her kind permission here, that led me (over a period of fifteen years, since the day I first read it) to the sentiment expressed in my own **Rule 11: Feel the fear, but dance anyway!**

Cecilia Sorochin of SoroDesign (**sorodesign.com**), who designed the beautiful cover I had always dreamed of, and thus gave **Happy Tango** its relaxed and smiling face. Jeff Barry of SoroDesign, who generously shared his knowledge of the print-on-demand publishing model and introduced me to Lightning Source (**lightningsource.com**), the company supplying the printing and distribution services for the book.

The soul of the special public space that is the Glorieta Barrancas de Belgrano, where we shot the book's cover photographs, and where I danced my first ever blissful tangos in Buenos Aires.

And last but by no means least, my friend Julie Michelle Sparenberg (**juliemichellephotography.com**), who sent me her own very first book of photographs, all the way to Argentina from San Francisco, and told me that I could do it too. Without Julie, who believed in me even though she had never met me, I'm not sure that one word of **Happy Tango** would ever have been written. Julie was the first angel.

Happy Tango

Table of Contents

Introduction

WHY HAPPY TANGO?

Flying in from abroad to dance in Buenos Aires is the stuff of dreams for any lover of Argentine tango: dancing with the best, learning at the source, going to the most famous and traditional tango salóns in the world. However, if you're on your own, know no-one in town, and are unfamiliar with the local tango scene, then the early days of the adventure might be a little daunting. Don't you think?

When I arrived, in March 2007, fresh from a quiet housewife life in the English countryside, a five-month-old baby in tango, and alone in Argentina, I had many questions and no answers. I longed for a tango buddy: a friendly and experienced *tanguera* or *tanguero* (lady or gent, passionate about tango) who could prepare me for what was to come; who could hold my hand at my first Argentine *milongas*; who could show me a way through the maze that is Buenos Aires tango.

The scale of it all presents a giant challenge: where, from the more than one hundred *milongas* in any given week, will you choose to dance? Then there's what to expect from a tango culture different from your own... all those *códigos*, *cortinas* and *cabeceos*, plus the pitfalls that can trip up the first-time tango tourist. All you know is that you're after the happiest possible Buenos Aires tango experiences. If this sounds like you, you have come to the right place.

I've danced in this city of tango dreams for several years. I've observed *mucho*, journeyed *mucho*, and learned *muchísimo*, and my lessons have not only been about dancing. Tango has given me the chance to find out who I really am. I've discovered that I'm a joyful soul who wants to encourage others on to a path of joy too. I've also noticed that when tango tourists aren't having a happy time here, I can usually help them back to smiles by telling them something I know, such as a place that might suit them, or a *cabeceo* trick they didn't know about, or a tip to stay late at the *milonga* to land the best dances of the night. I got to thinking, *What if I could give tango tourists all that useful stuff, in a book?* The intention for **Happy Tango** was born.

Happy Tango is a definitive slice of Buenos Aires tango: it's what I know to be true today (things change fast around here). If I'd had this book in my hand back in 2007, I'd have saved myself a lot of time, a lot of tears and a lot of complaints. I know it can do the same for you. It'll probably do most for you if you've already got a decent bit of Argentine tango under your belt in your own country and you're coming to Buenos Aires for the first time. But even if you've never danced a step or if Buenos Aires is no more than a mirage in your tango dreams, **Happy Tango** is going to set you firmly on the path of understanding the adventure that could lie ahead. Perhaps it might even inspire you to start dancing in the direction of Argentina. That'd be cool.

Just to be one hundred percent clear, the tango in **Happy Tango** is improvised. It's an intimate dance created in the moment by two tango dancers interpreting tango music and dancing only for one another (and not for an audience), usually at a social dance event known as a *milonga*. It has little in common with the flashy split-skirt-and-fishnets choreographed tango dished up on TV outside of Argentina, on Buenos

Aires dinner-show stages or on the street corners of the more touristic districts of the city. In **Why I Dance Tango in Buenos Aires** I reveal what Argentine tango can mean to me. If you are seeking even an ounce of what I describe there, this book can lead you to it.

Happy Tango means dancing. It means finding dance partners who can offer you bliss. It means offering your partners the same in return. In Buenos Aires, I have found that I am most likely to dance blissful tango when I follow **Sallycat's Rules for Happy Tango in Buenos Aires**, outlined in **Part 1**.

Happy Tango means feeling relaxed and confident in the Buenos Aires tango experience. **Part 2: The A to Z of Dancing Tango in Buenos Aires** tells you everything you need to know in order to fit in from the start.

Happy Tango means dancing in places where you feel most comfortable. **Part 3: Where Will You Dance in Buenos Aires?** helps you to decide where you should dance first, and gives you the lowdown on twenty of your potential 'tango homes', in three broad categories: Tourist-circuit, Traditional and Informal. Those twenty places will lead you to many more.

Happy Tango means not having to sweat the small stuff, and being free to focus on dancing instead. **Part 4: Buenos Aires Practicalities for Tango Dancers** covers the basics of life in this city. Which district to stay in, how to get around, what the food's like; I explain it all. I even give you a few options for exploring the sights when you decide to take some time off tango, which you absolutely must!

And finally, in **The Future of *Happy Tango***, I tell you where you can find updates to this second edition of the book as time passes and things change in Buenos Aires, as they inevitably will. My methods have worked well during the two years since the first edition of the book was published, and it is my intention to continue to use them in an attempt to keep ***Happy Tango*** readers well informed.

May adventure and discovery and joy in tango and in life be yours.

Sallycat

Why I Dance Tango In Buenos Aires

I originally wrote a version of this essay, on the theme of 'Destination unknown', for the *Independent on Sunday/Bradt Travel-Writing Competition 2009*. It was shortlisted, reaching the final six. It didn't win, but I think it conveys what tango can be for me, and why I love to dance in Argentina. Will you find something of this bliss on your Buenos Aires tango journey? I hope you do.

T-Time In Buenos Aires

My cab is stuck to the asphalt of Corrientes like its tyres are melting in the thirty-five degree heat. The Obelisco looms up from its restless bed in the centre of Avenida 9 de Julio. Horns hit my ears. The aircon blast can't mask the stale drift of cigarette from my *taxista*'s clothes, as he shifts to stare back at me. He's just found out I'm British, speak enough *Castellano* to reveal all, and he's hot on the trail of Lady 'Dee': *A conspiracy? What about the wicked Prince? The other woman?* My answers flow pat, the minutes tick slow, and the meter racks up, but I can bear it this afternoon: my mind is on the new four-inch stiletto heels in my bag.

On the pavement opposite Suipacha 384, I look up. I always do. The suspended sign that will glow red neon by night; the broken windows that cannot keep the beckoning melodies from the street; the stone balcony on which I have stood, and smoked, and caught my breath so many times. I delay. Buy mints at the *kiosko*. Drag out the seconds until I will mount the stairs and allow the music to drown out the background chatter of my life. It's my ritual: a calming; a buffer zone between the chaotic and bliss.

The steps to the first floor are worn to shallow smiles. Who has climbed them across the decades? Pugliese on the way to his piano keys; Pablo Veron en route to stardom; Sally Potter blazing the trail, the likes of me in her wake; and the strangers who now, this minute, wait to take me in their arms. A gust of hot wind blows the balcony curtain towards me as I pass, a caress of wine red velvet on my hand. I push my $15 pesos across the smooth counter of wood and exchange kisses with the hostess.

You're late, I thought you weren't coming. How was your week? Are you alone today? I am. She guides me to my table, although I know it as a home: the layered cream and *vino tinto* coloured cloths scarred by cigarette burns and flung into unruly folds by the draughts from the huge wall fans; the two crimson leather chairs with their buttock-dented seats; the marble column around which I will have to peer with determination, to catch the farthest male eyes.

I do not look up as I prepare. Instead, I keep my gaze on my Cinderella slippers as they slide out of their silk bag. I focus only on my transformation, slip naked feet into silver metallic snake-skin, adjust tiny buckles and thin straps, flex my ankles awake: unseen below the cloak of the tablecloth. The waiter appears, all bow tie and apron, and I order my *agua con gas* and a *cortado*: coffee will heighten my senses and the water will cool me. I place my fan on the table. Adjust the clip in my hair. Finally I'm ready. I raise my eyes.

On the smooth polished stone, pairs of bodies weave their unique and silent songs. Each embrace carries two hearts and two souls in its arms. Music transports the soul. The soul directs the feet. The feet dance.

I see my regular gentlemen: I already know where we will walk together today. I linger over the men who I've never touched: how will it be to lean into their chests, their heartbeats, the voices of their dance? The clues undulate before me and I search them out: a body shape, a height, a hand touching a back, the smoothness of a step, an expression on a partner's face, even the way he escorts her from the floor when the *tanda* ends with the shock of rock 'n' roll. I hold each man in my gaze, one after the other, and I smile because I find him quite easily today: the stranger I will accept if the music insists that I take a risk, and his eyes find mine.

The first notes of a De Angelis *tanda* surge into five o'clock and I decide. My eyes do not leave him as he sips his glass of champagne. He looks up, and straight at me. I glance away. I put down my fan. I glance back. His stare is constant. Me. He wants me too. He inclines his head. Slowly and deliberately, I nod my acceptance. He stands and begins his walk towards me. I take off my glasses: I know that for the next four tangos he is mine. I am about to discover the story of an unknown soul.

Warning

SALLYCAT SPANGLISH

It's only fair to warn you: there's a bit of Spanglish in **Happy Tango**. I use plenty of beautiful Spanish words as I write. These I put in italics, and unless their meaning is completely obvious, at the first convenient opportunity, I define them. Like this:

... if you're desperate, take a trip to the *baños* (toilets/restrooms).

Once I've given you the definition, I get rid of the italics and use them as Spanglish. Like this:

... if you're still desperate, take a trip to the baños.

I do this because some words, such as *cabeceo* (in tango, meaning the nod-of-the-head invitation — and the acceptance — to dance), are used so often in this book that if I wrote them in italics every time, it would drive you completely crazy. I reckon this isn't too tricky to follow, because I swap noun for noun and verb for verb, in true Spanglish style. And who knows, my method might even help you learn a bit of Spanish.

But when it comes to the cabeceo, the Sallycat Spanglish does get a little more dangerous, I confess. *El* (the) cabeceo is a noun, you see, but occasionally in this book, I use it as a verb. Why? First off, it's how I tend to talk in English, in Buenos Aires, when faced with wonderfully clever words in Spanish that just don't exist as one simple equivalent word in my own language. And, although the verb *cabecear* (in tango, meaning to perform the cabeceo) exists, the truth is that I, like many native English speakers, tend to say things like:

If you want to cabeceo someone from your seat... rather than:
If you want to cabecear someone from your seat...

Words like cabeceo-ed and cabeceo-ing can crop up in conversation too. It might not be quite grammatically correct, but we do it to communicate more efficiently and easily, and that's what I want to do in **Happy Tango**. So occasionally, I'll be teaching you how to cabeceo rather than cabecear, and you'll understand exactly what I mean.

Claro (Right)?

Part 1

SALLYCAT'S RULES FOR HAPPY TANGO IN BUENOS AIRES

I've got eleven (Sallycat's lucky number) rules for my tango sessions in Buenos Aires. They're born of bittersweet experience. They're mine. When I follow them, I leave the milonga smiling. When I forget even one, I can cause myself all kinds of problems.

At first glance The Rules make a degree of sense, but might not seem really important. By the time you've read this book, you'll be in no doubt as to why they're the key to happy dancing experiences. I will explain the why, the when and the how of each. There can be exceptions to every rule, of course, and I'll be pointing those out too.

The Rules

1: **Only accept or invite a person you have observed dancing.**

2: **Women — don't accept a verbal invitation unless you know the person or he is Pablo Veron[1].
Men — use the cabeceo.**

3: **Seek out your 'tango homes'.**

4: **Exude magnetic energy.**

5: **Look the part.**

6: **Work the room.**

7: **Leave your expectations behind.**

8: **Be realistic.**

9: **Know that you can say *No*.**

10: **Stay late. Go back.**

11: **Feel the fear, but dance anyway!**

Understanding The Rules

You'll find The Rules referenced again and again throughout **Part 2** and **Part 3**. Here are the basics to get you started.

Rule 1: Only accept or invite a person you have observed dancing.

Two facts you have to know about tango in Buenos Aires:

1. Not everyone is a fabulous dancer... or even a half-fabulous dancer.
2. It's polite to dance the whole *tanda* (set, normally of four tangos), with any partner you have invited or accepted (unless a serious offence occurs).

---

[1] I've picked Pablo Veron (star of Sally Potter's 1997 film **The Tango Lesson** by Sony Pictures), but ladies, you can insert any famous or non-famous male tango dancer's name, preferably one you wouldn't be able to resist sharing a tanda with, even if he invited you to do so by dragging you to your feet by your hair.

You need to ensure you land a partner whose tango embrace you will be happy to share until the *cortina* (tanda break). When possible, observe the dancers first, make informed partner choices, and up your chances of finding Happy Tango in the arms of someone who can actually dance.

Are there exceptions to this rule? Of course. You get a good vibe from someone; you want to be kind-hearted and give a start to a newbie who hasn't yet left his or her seat; you can't observe because the layout of the venue makes it impossible; you like taking risks; you're desperate to dance. I understand. I like to live a little dangerously too — sometimes.

Rule 2: Women — don't accept a verbal invitation unless you know the person or he is Pablo Veron. Men — use the cabeceo.

A few Argentine men, who can't dance tango at all and/or whose prime objective is something other than dancing (in the worst cases, groping), ignore the cabeceo etiquette and use a verbal invitation instead. These guys rely on the following three facts:

1. Newbie females are likely to accept a verbal invitation from any Argentine male, out of relief that someone is asking them to dance and because they may have heard that 'if you refuse an invitation from an Argentine, he'll never ask you again'.
2. Polite foreign ladies will be too embarrassed to refuse face-to-face verbal invitations.
3. Foreigners may initially prefer the verbal invitation to the cabeceo because verbal invitations are the norm in their own countries.

By the time tourist women cotton on to this neat trick and begin to appreciate the power of refusal granted to them by the cabeceo, they've gained a line of these guys (the men I call bottom feeders), and have to work out how to ditch them fast. Tourist males who don't want to get mixed up in this little game can avoid it and resist putting any unwelcome pressure on the ladies, by using the cabeceo. Argentine women expect the cabeceo in all but the more Informal (see **Part 3** for my definition of Informal) venues, and even in these many might prefer it. The cabeceo leads to Happy Tango because it gives choice without pressure or awkwardness to both men and women.

Pablo Veron, perhaps along with guys you know well, might be the exception to this rule, and you can find out more under **Verbal invitation**, in **Part 2**.

Rule 3: Seek out your 'tango homes'.

If you want Happy Tango experiences fast, go to the places that are most likely to suit and satisfy you: the style of tango you want to dance, the venue-vibe that turns you on, the people you want to mix with. **Part 3: Where Will You Dance in Buenos Aires?** is going to help you with that.

Rule 4: Exude magnetic energy.

The single most important factor in having a brilliant night out on the Buenos Aires tango scene is the energy we exude. Whichever venue we are in, wherever our seat is located, however many wrinkles we have got... if our energy is flat and ugly we won't dance much. If our energy zings with life we might not sit down all night.

I used to blame a bad night (sitting for hours and rarely dancing) on stuff outside of me — the lack of dances in the first half an hour, the specs on my face, the supermodel in the row in front of me. But then I noticed that it was the effect those outside factors had on me that explained the problem. After all, would I want to dance with a miserable looking foreigner who was shrinking into her seat, while scowling, complaining and tapping her foot impatiently against the table leg?

I'm attracted to the guys who look interested, interesting and awake, even at 4am. In the milongas of Buenos Aires, magnetic energy attracts, and negative energy repels. And, with respect to this rule, there are no exceptions. Sorry! There may always be some aspect of a night out that you can complain has stopped you getting the Happy Tango experience you wanted, but just make sure it isn't you.

Rule 5: Look the part.

The right glad rags are essential for men and women: elegance, glamour, sex-appeal... do your best to dress for success and draw the most desirable eyes. When you look fabulous and behave without causing offence, you will attract the right kind of interest and thus increase the probability of happy nights on the tango town.

Rule 6: Work the room.

Contrary to the understanding of most first-time tango tourists, the cabeceo is a very active sport for both men and women. New men in town might think that from their seat, they are the ones to fix a woman in their sights and invite her with a nod. New women in town might know that the men make the invitation. So, both parties sit in their seats all night, the men stare purposefully at their targets, and the women vaguely scan the rows of men hoping to notice eyes focused in their direction. Right?

No, there's much more to it than that. You both have work to do. Boys, yours may involve getting up and moving around the room in order to widen your cabeceo options. Girls, yours includes informed choices, determined stares (known as *miradas*, meaning looks) and small movements that attract attention. In a Buenos Aires milonga, you have to do all you can to increase your chances of dancing both with those sitting yards away, and with those seated on the far side of the dance floor. So you need to 'work the room' to the max for potential cabeceos, and those who do will find themselves with a greater number of potential tango partners and thus more chances of Happy Tango.

Rule 7: Leave your expectations behind.

Come here with big ideas of what Buenos Aires tango should be, and you'll probably find out it isn't like that at all. You risk disappointment. Disappointment leads to complaints. Complaints lead to negative energy. Negative energy is the opposite of magnetic energy. Things can only get worse. Worse does not make for Happy Tango.

My expectations of Buenos Aires tango were based on what I had learned about tango in my own country, often from my own country-men. My expectations were laced with my cultural background, my social conditioning and my values. Argentine tango in Buenos Aires, danced socially by the locals on a Saturday night in the more Traditional (see **Part 3** for my definition of Traditional) venues, offered up a few surprises... but truthfully, when I stopped to think about it for five se-conds, nothing was really that surprising. This is Argentina, a land far removed from mine, and I did come here to learn something about *Argentine* tango, after all. I think I'd have been a bit disappointed if I'd found nothing outside of my own rather limited British experience.

Come here with an open mind and a willingness to explore what is, ask why it is what it is, reflect on why it is what it is... hell, even writing this I can feel the difference in energy. Enjoy the exploration of the new and different, and everyone else will feel your up energy too — the people you want to dance with, the people who sit next to you in the milongas, even the people you pass in the street on the way to the milonga. Your tango experience will be affected by the expectations you bring to it. Dump your preconceptions at the airport, and your chances of Happy Tango will rise, fast.

Rule 8: Be realistic.

Even if you're a Tango God or Goddess back home, unless you are already well known on the Buenos Aires tango scene or have famous or well-known tango friends here, it might take the locals a bit of time to spot your deity status. You'll have to be seen dancing, be seen to be in the know, be seen to stay late and go back, just like the rest of us. A healthy dose of realism will be needed in other departments too: even Tango Gods and Goddesses have ups and downs, and even with this book in your hand you might not avoid all the pitfalls. How does being realistic lead to Happy Tango? Well, for me it's the balance that reminds me that everyone we meet on our tango journey is human, that every situation we come across is created by human beings, and that there may be tears on the way as well as laughter. Keep this in mind, and when the occasional blows to your ego come, you'll be ready for them and they'll feel softer.

Rule 9: Know that you can say *No*.

Back in my home country, I was brought up in a tango scene where it was frowned upon to say no to an invitation to dance. In my local milongas, I was even able to verbally invite men, and they were under equal pressure to accept me. It doesn't work like that here. In Buenos Aires, where the men ask the women and not the other way round, we girls say no if we don't want to dance. With the cabeceo *código* (etiquette), it's as easy as a look in the other direction. With a verbal invitation, it's as easy as two words: *No, gracias.* In some venues, if you say yes to everyone who asks you, you'll end up regretting it: you'll find yourself dancing with the bottom feeders, the worst dancers in the room, the guys no-one else wants to embrace. It won't make for Happy Tango. Girls, if you're not used to saying no, toughen up and get used to it. Boys, if you're not used to being refused, toughen up and get used to it. In Buenos Aires it's the norm and nothing to get hung up about. I've come to find the whole thing rather refreshing. If I don't want to dance, I say no. The men have the power to choose who to invite (and let's face it, by not inviting in the first place, they are effectively saying no). The women have the power to refuse. Fair's fair. Fair's Happy Tango.

Rule 10: Stay late. Go back.

Stay late! The best part of the night for newcomers often comes at the end: the crowd thins out and instead of being a new face lost in a sea of regulars, you become a point of interest visible from across the room; the dance floor clears and your dancing can be seen and appreciated by those wondering whether to risk someone new; the regulars might have exhausted their own regular partners and be willing to take a chance on you. You might have to push through the tiredness barrier at around 3am and stoke your magnetic energy with a *café doble*, but so many times when I have done exactly that, I've gone on to land my Happiest Tangos of the night. Plus, demonstration of commitment gets rewarded in Tangoland Buenos Aires where the regulars rule. Even two nights at the same milonga makes you more of a regular than you were the first time you visited. So if you want more Happy Tangos, don't just stay late — go back next week!

Rule 11: Feel the fear, but dance anyway!

New situations set the pulse racing, don't they? And first-time Buenos Aires tango experiences are no exception. Trying to land my first successful cabeceo by staring strange men straight in the eye, not understanding a single word that was said to me between tangos on the dance floor, heading alone to a milonga full of strangers at midnight... butterflies in my tummy, anxiety, terror — in the beginning I had them all, every night. Not any more. I felt the fear, but did it all anyway, and now those unfamiliar experiences have become familiar and my fears have flown. Want to land successful cabeceos? Do it. Want to speak *Castellano* (the brand of Castilian Spanish spoken in Buenos Aires)? Do it. Want to dance in the most famous milongas in Argentina? Do it. There's only one way to make the tango world of your dreams a reality, and that's to walk in it. Scared or not, do it. Dance over your fears. They will shrink, and you can replace them with Happy Tango memories.

Part 2

THE A TO Z OF DANCING TANGO IN BUENOS AIRES

This is the part where you can look up all the stuff you want to know about tango in Buenos Aires, and where I tell you the things you don't yet know you need to know. Overleaf are the A to Z topics in alphabetical order on one handy page, so you can see if there's anything you fancy checking out first, or you can tick them off when you've seen them in action or tried them yourself. Along the way, I'll be mentioning lots of places to dance tango in Buenos Aires — you'll be able to find more details of them all, in **Part 3**.

THE A TO Z TOPICS

Adventure	Afternoons	Age
Bailás?	Baños	Be seen
Beginners	Besitos	Bliss
Bottom feeders	Cabeceo	Cameras
Classes	Coat check	Códigos
Coffee invite	Cortina	Couples
Crowds	Dance floors	Disappointment
Dress for success	Entrada	Exhibitions
Famous	Food and drink	Gay-friendly tango
Group classes	Hosts and organisers	Knowledge matters
Live orchestras	Love hotels	Lovers
Milongueros	Music	Navigation
No, gracias	Non-tango tandas	Observation
Private classes	Regular or tourist?	Reservations
Seating	Serious offence	Shoe change
Shoe shopping	Sitting out	Smoking
Solo dancers	Sorteo	Styles of tango
Tanda	Tango schools	Taxi dancers
Unwanted attention	Valuables	Verbal invitation
	Zapatos	

Adventure

I first heard the words 'Argentine tango' in a slightly seedy bar in Ulaan Baatar, Mongolia, in the summer of 2006, when I was forty-three years old. Within nine months and with only five months of UK tango under my belt, I flew to Buenos Aires, determined to become a great dancer. I took tango lessons with Ariel Yanovsky (see **Sallycat's Tango Teacher** at the end of the book). I met *mi amor* Carlos in La Glorieta, one of the city's most romantic tango venues. I ended up following my heart and staying on in Argentina, where I gradually exchanged wanting to *be* a great tango dancer, for longing to *feel* great (both for myself and for my partners) when I dance. I get more cabeceos than I did, so perhaps I'm getting there. My journey to Buenos Aires started with tango. Now it's about learning to live between two lands, write books and turn dreams into reality. Adventure? Oh yes.

Welcome to yours!

Afternoons

Want to cut your tango teeth before heading out into the Buenos Aires night? Do it in the afternoons and early evenings at the matinée milongas. They're less intimidating, less competitive and they cost less dosh.

Where to start? Well, as afternoon venues go, the least scary place of all has to be Confitería Ideal. I know there are downsides: a few bottom feeders; one or two teachers handing you a business card after the tanda (to be expected in a venue that attracts so many tourists, but it can be a surprise the first time it happens); and you will probably find yourself dancing in the camera lenses of non-tanguero sightseeing spectators. But Ideal is kind to unfamiliar faces. Women are likely to be invited to dance by Argentines and foreigners, and men are likely to be accepted. You will find regulars, and tourists passing through, who can dance — it's your job to spot who they are (and this in itself is good practice). There are additional bonuses too: on quieter days, there is space on the dance floor; the venue is super-historic and offers an atmosphere worth soaking up; and there's a balcony for smoking or a gulp of fresh air, depending on your preference. This balcony has been one of my favourite places, for chatting with tango-dancing strangers, for looking down on Suipacha and Corrientes, and for punching the air (when no-one's looking) and yelling *I'm here!* It's a great place to escape to for a moment and regroup if confidence is low. If you employ a few of The Rules at La Ideal, you can ease yourself into Buenos Aires tango in a relaxed environment. Work on following **Rule 1: Only accept or invite a person you have observed dancing**, and **Rule 2: Women — don't accept a verbal invitation unless you know the person or he is Pablo Veron. Men — use the cabeceo.**

Other afternoon/early-evening spots I have tried and enjoyed are the El Arranque milongas in Nuevo Salón La Argentina, La Milonga de los Consagrados in Centro Región Leonesa, A Puro Tango in Salón Canning, Lujos in El Beso and Nuevo Chiqué in Casa de Galicia. All are on the Traditional side, but are fairly relaxed and it's certainly possible for new faces in town to dance with the locals. In the case of Lujos in El Beso on Thursdays, it's good to go early, as the more high-powered regulars arrive later on, and your chances of dancing are likely to diminish if you are an unfamiliar face. You'll also get a better seat.

Age

Does it matter? You will certainly see the results of cosmetic surgery in the milongas, but do you need to get some before you come? I'm forty-nine, am no supermodel, wear specs, and in my experience, I think age can matter. How much though, depends in part on you.

First off, the tango scene in Buenos Aires loves its oldies; the music and dance maestros now in their seventies, eighties and nineties are celebrated and adored. In any Traditional milonga you'll see men and women out to party regardless of their age, and I'm convinced that I will be able to attend milongas when I have white hair and will still be made to feel welcome. On the other hand, the number of dances I'll get if I choose to turn up at Milonga10 when I'm in my dotage will be another matter entirely.

Most of the Argentine men who ask me to dance in the more Traditional milongas and in the Tourist-circuit (see **Part 3** for my definition of Tourist-circuit) places are significantly older than I am. Younger foreigners or Argentines visiting from out of town will pick me too, if they've seen me dance. However, in general, the younger men go for the younger women. In the more Informal venues that have a far lower average age, I rarely get invited to dance by the more youthful crowd, be they locals or foreigners.

If I was a twenty-something supermodel, I suspect I'd receive many more invitations from younger guys than I do, and surely that would be the case anywhere in the world. It's a male-female thing, not a Buenos Aires tango thing. I'd also attract a lot of types that I prefer to keep at arm's length: the guys who want something other than tango. So there are swings and roundabouts. I've got no complaints. And I won't be getting a facelift any time soon.

New girls in town, you can maximise your invitations to dance, whatever your age, if you employ **Rules 3: Seek out your 'tango homes', 4: Exude magnetic energy, 5: Look the part** and **6: Work the room**. If none of that works, then the ace up your sleeve has to be **Rule 10: Stay late. Go back**. Thus, fight the urge to leave when the going gets a bit disheartening, because the best often comes at the end of the night. If it doesn't, but you still feel determined to crack the place, you have no alternative except to return the following week and try again. Even two weeks in a row makes you more of a regular than on your first visit!

Middle-aged tango tourist males tell me that they can find it tough in some venues at first. Visiting female tangueras can be keenest to dance with Argentines, and the local women have their regulars. Boys, you will need to follow the exact same rules too. The good news is that you have an option for **Rule 6: Work the room** that we girls do not (see **Be seen** and **Cabeceo** for more details).

The trick, whatever your age, is to feel comfortable and confident in the venues you visit, behave in ways that show you are in the know, dress for success, and relax. And follow **Rule 8: Be realistic**, but don't go overboard by being pessimistic. I have learned that I can be quick to blame my age or my looks when I don't get the dances I want, but I'm not sure that's fair: magnetic energy can refresh the parts that anti-wrinkle creams cannot. Believe in it, exude it and dance!

Ballás?

It means *Do you dance?* or *Would you like to dance?* and the answer will not always be *Sí*. Sometimes you are going to want to say *No, gracias*, and in Buenos Aires you can. In the more Traditional venues, where the cabeceo is the norm, a woman is unlikely to be asked to dance verbally, but a man silently might mouth *Bailás?* as part of his invitation from afar, when he is certain the woman will accept. A variation is *Bailamos?* (Shall we dance?).

Querés bailar? (Do you want to dance?) might be used as a verbal invitation in some of the Tourist-circuit and Informal places and in the outdoor venues.

Baños

Always take a few pesos with you to the toilets, because in the busier Tourist-circuit venues and the more popular milongas there will be an attendant handing out toilet paper and paper-towels and a tip is expected. Usually there's a saucer with a few $2, $5 or $10 peso notes on display to give you the hint. Do be kind and polite to the attendants; they are interesting people and a part of the tango world. Don't be surprised to find some restrooms are more like shops, with sweets, condoms, CDs, postcards and even tango clothes on sale (yes, in some Tourist-circuit places you can nip to the loo and return to your seat in a new outfit if you wish). Most have a chair where you can change into your tango shoes. However, don't expect luxury in the bathroom department: be prepared for door locks that don't work, water on the floor, and toilets that can't cope with paper, which has to go into a bin instead. If you want to keep your hands clean at all times, regardless of the state of the baños, carry alcohol hand rub or wet wipes in your bag.

Women's toilets may be signed *Damas (D)*, *Mujeres (M)* or *Ellas*, and the men's *Caballeros (C)*, *Hombres (H)* or *Ellos*.

Castellano you might need:

Perdón, dónde está el baño? — Excuse me, where is the toilet/restroom?

Gracias — Thank you.

Be seen

If you want to dance, you need to be seen.

Tango dancers in Buenos Aires who care about their reputation and seek joy from their dancing experiences, normally won't risk dancing with a new face unless they have first seen them dance. Thus, if you know somebody at the milonga who'll invite or accept you early on in the session, you're off to a flying start: someone you met in a group class, someone you danced with at another milonga, your partner if you are in a couple or a taxi dancer. If the watching dancers like what they see, they may seek you out later.

What if you know no-one and you're not getting any dances? You need to make yourself more visible. This is where **Rule 6: Work the room** comes in, because the longer you remain like a statue in your seat, the more invisible you become. Here's what you can do:

•   Men, if there is room to move and you see other men doing the same, you can get up and walk to a fresh vantage point — the bar, an aisle, a corner, an unoccupied seat. As you walk or once you arrive, you can spot potential partners, and if they catch your eye, you have the option to invite, from a standing position.
•   Women, get up and go to the restroom, out to the balcony for a breath of fresh air, or out for a smoke (if you do). Walk with confidence, eye the men, and let them see you.
•   Women who are sitting and not dancing much, remember **Rule 4: Exude magnetic energy**. Have a brief conversation with the person

next to you. Laugh. Toss your hair. Shift your sitting position. Sit up straight. Creating even a little movement at the table can catch somebody's eye. Of course I'm not suggesting that you move about so much that you start to look like you've got ants in your tango-pants or that you elbow anyone in your efforts to energise yourself, but don't let disappointment sink you further and further into your seat and make you less and less visible. Your first dance of the night could be as close as a smile in the right direction.

Rule 5: Look the part is vital for everyone trying to be seen — and this you have to think about before you even leave home for the milonga, though you sure can learn a lot from observation once you're there, for next time. For advice on what to wear to help you get noticed and remembered, check out the tips in **Dress for success**.

Beginners

If you are an absolute beginner in tango, that is to say you have never danced a step of it in your life or you have only a few classes under your belt, do take some classes in Buenos Aires and spend time observing other dancers in the milongas before you take to the dance floors mentioned in this book. Look for group classes that advertise as being for *principiantes* (beginners), or consider finding a private teacher who can teach excellent fundamentals. I offer you **10 Tango Schools** in **Appendix A**, and most run classes for beginners. Visit any that appeal to you, try a principiantes class in each and see which suit you best; this can also be a great way to discover a private teacher, as most people teaching group classes give private lessons. In the same way that **Rule 3: Seek out your 'tango homes'** works for places to dance, a similar strategy also works for tango teachers, tango classes and tango schools. We each have different needs and desires, and you will have to find out what is right for you (see **Group classes**, **Private classes** and **Tango schools** for more information).

Ask your teachers to help you decide when you might be ready to dance in a milonga or a public *práctica* (in theory, a práctica is an informal dance event where it might be acceptable to practise your tango, or try out things you've learned in class; but in Buenos Aires, some public prácticas can feel as high-powered as the milongas, and it really isn't appropriate to hold up the flow of dance while you work out a new step with your partner). For a less intimidating experience, some tango schools run prácticas for their students, and these can be brilliant places to take to the floor among friends and try out what you have learned. These prácticas give leaders the opportunity to navigate a dance floor populated by other couples, as well as allowing everyone to dance in a supportive and tolerant environment.

Even the more experienced beginners, well on their way to improver level, may find many of the public prácticas and milongas mentioned in this book a bit daunting. Most tango venues in Buenos Aires assume a certain level of knowledge and skill. Men must be able to dance and navigate the floor to a standard that will keep their partners and other dancers safe; women need to be capable of following most leads reasonably competently — one or two errors in a tango may be acceptable, too many more might feel embarrassing with a new partner; couples need to be dancing with a degree of skill that ensures they will not impede other dancers. It's not about being perfect. Everyone makes mistakes. I occasionally misstep; my partner may accidentally nudge another couple on a crowded floor; sometimes we just don't click and things don't work out too well. However, if you become aware that you are the cause of repeated problems on the dance floor, and/or your confidence is low, then it would be better to seek out dance spaces appropriate for practising or to watch for a while. Leaders, if you do find yourself surrounded by dancers more skilled than you are, stay towards the middle of the floor: the more advanced will stick to the outer lines of dance. Keep your partner safe, keep moving in a counter-clockwise direction and don't cut across other couples or obstruct the flow.

When you are ready to try the public prácticas and milongas, it's a good idea to turn up early, when there'll be more space to dance without disturbing anyone else; as the floor fills, you can sit out and watch. If you're not in a couple or you haven't come to Buenos Aires with a group, then you could make friends in the tango schools and in the classes before the milongas and prácticas. If you are new on the scene, it is

...ways an excellent idea to do these group classes and then stay on to dance during the quieter, first hour. Later, you can sit back, enjoy the music and learn from observing (as I have done for many hours, I assure you), even if you don't get many dances.

Informal La Viruta can be a fun place to start. The more highly skilled dancers arrive in the early hours of the morning, so earlier on, immediately after the classes, there's a more tolerant vibe that can suit improvers. The bohemian venue La Catedral is a funky space for practising with a partner: take one of the classes and stay on, eat some vegetarian food and dance a little before the floor becomes too crowded. Outdoors, La Glorieta can be a good option, as it attracts a wide range of dance levels and is relaxed, but it gets busy later — so arrive early; when the dance floor starts filling up, you can always take advantage of the music and practise on the paved area around the bandstand (although it's stone, and lumpy and bumpy, so ladies would definitely need flat shoes). The prácticas held at Cochabamba 444, San Telmo, have been favourites with improver-level friends of mine, serious about practising their social tango, and offer the chance to try a more intimate venue with a non-intimidating atmosphere. On the more Traditional side, Confitería Ideal is the most forgiving place to begin, especially in the afternoons.

I'd been learning to dance tango for only five months when I arrived in Buenos Aires. I coped in the milongas here because, although I made many errors on the dance floor, the Argentine men were very kind to me. Some of them did try to teach me between tangos. Others repeatedly told me to relax, which knocked my confidence a bit. And in my ignorance about which venues were high-powered, I went everywhere and dealt with the blows to my ego when no-one picked me. In the matter of how long you should wait before taking to the milonga floor, beginner women definitely have it easier than men: I imagine that it's far more straightforward to follow in the arms of an accomplished leader on a Buenos Aires dance floor than it is to lead anyone at all. Even if you come as a couple planning to dance only with each other, it will be the skills of the leader that will decide whether you are up to dancing in the milongas or not.

Besitos

El Beso (one of the most famous and centrally located Traditional-style tango venues in Buenos Aires) is named The Kiss, and aptly so. I feel as if I've received more *besitos* (little kisses) since first arriving in Buenos Aires than in my entire pre-Argentina life.

Expect a single kiss-on-the-right-cheek greeting, even among total strangers, and between men. Use *Un beso, besos* or *bs* to represent kisses at the end of informal emails and text messages (a written 'x' has no significance as a kiss in Argentina). Say *Te mando un beso* (I send you a kiss) at the end of phone calls to friends and acquaintances. And, be warned that rounds of friendly goodbye kisses can prolong your departure from any decent-sized gathering of Argentines by tens of minutes.

Having got used to socialising in Argentina, I can't help but notice how distant many foreign tourists appear, when they rather stiffly hold out their hand to me on a first meeting. I hereby apologise to anyone I've surprised with my newly learned behaviour of enthusiastic hugs and pecks on the cheek. No-one else in Buenos Aires means to surprise you with their penchant for kissing either, and now that I've warned you, they won't have to, and you can be ready to kiss them right back.

Having said all that, however, I've noticed that in the case of tango encounters on the dance floor, unless I know the man already, I am not usually greeted with a kiss of any kind. Rather, sometimes there isn't even a *Hola* or a hint of a smile. It is as if entering the tango embrace itself is the greeting, the hug and the meeting. It's only when we break away after the first tango that the smiles and conversation come.

Bliss

We foreigners come to dance in Buenos Aires (and endure many setbacks along the way) because sometimes we discover something close to bliss. Here are five things that give me bliss; your own may overlap with some of them, or may come from other experiences:

1.   The embrace: the best that an Argentine man can offer enables a tango connection that I could never have imagined even in my dreams; I feel secure, treasured, beautiful, loved, cared for, warm, wrapped in a duvet, hugged and rather dizzy afterwards (visiting men don't seem to experience this in quite the same way; an intriguing subject for a future book, perhaps?).

2.   The love of tango music that my favourite Argentine partners transmit to me: they speak of it in the breaks between tangos; they sing snippets in my ear; they let me feel it from their hearts as they dance.

3.   The atmospheric venues: the historic and Traditional are my personal favourites; most have tables around the dance floor, food and drink available, and waiter service, all of which I appreciate, as I like to feel a little pampered on my tango nights out.

4.   The live orchestras, some with tango singers, that play in many venues: a treat every time.

5.   The microcosm of life that unfolds before my eyes in the milongas. I never grow tired of watching the locals, the tourists, the foreigners, the new faces, the regulars and the famous. There's the fashion parade that instructs me in what never to wear; the barely visible signals between men and women that offer me a masterclass in the cabeceo; the grace and elegance of the most experienced dancers in the room, who show me how to dance and how to behave. There can be drama too. I've witnessed a fight break out on a famous *pista* (dance floor). I've watched spats over seats. I've seen countless cabeceo cock-ups, inappropriate displays of show tango on packed floors, collisions. But more than anything, I love to study the facial expressions, the characters, and the people that the milonga attracts. All this is the world of tango Buenos Aires, and I feel privileged to sit and dance in its midst.

Other visitors are mesmerised by the quality of the best teachers and come to take classes or seminars with the maestros they worship from a distance all year round. Or they choose their milongas based on the exhibitions on offer: they want to see their tango idols dance in public, in grand or famous spaces such as Salón Canning and Club Sunderland. Some foreigners tell me that Buenos Aires attracts the best dancers from all over the world and that they don't need to dance with Argentines: the brilliant foreign dancers do it for them. Some love that they can dance virtually 24/7 if they want to. I love that too — it's not that I *do*, it's that I *can*!

But is a Buenos Aires tango journey always going to be blissful? Overall mine has been, but along the way there have been many downs as well as ups. Sometimes the downs have lasted hours, other times days. Yet I've persevered in my quest for bliss because I've always known that it exists here and that it's available to us all: I've watched others find it, and I've wanted it for myself. I've learned that as long as I dance in my 'tango homes', follow The Rules and know what to expect, bliss can be mine. And thus, especially with the information in this book in your hands, I believe that a little Buenos Aires tango bliss can be yours too.

Bottom feeders

These (fortunately, not too many) Argentine men hang out (mainly) in the Tourist-circuit places and prey on tourist women new in town. They know every face in the milongas they frequent and so they will know you are a newbie. They will approach you at your table, sometimes even before you've had a chance to put your shoes on, invite you verbally, and can even become a bit cross and make a fuss if you refuse them.

What are their motives? Well, I've watched a few of them operating and I think these guys fall into one, two and sometimes even two and a half of these three categories:

1. The men (and these are generally in the older age group) who can't dance tango at all, but who just want the opportunity to shuffle around the dance floor with a woman. They are usually harmless, but can leave you feeling awkward and embarrassed when you realise what you have landed: a shuffler, a plodder, an arm wrencher-offer or a person who can't follow the music at all. A tanda of four tangos can seem four years long with one of these boys.

2. The big ego 'experts' who want to give you a tango lesson, whether they can dance or not. It might be a patronising *Well done* after the first tango, but it could be an impromptu attempt to teach you mid-tango, between tangos or at the end of the tanda. It's rude to

start telling anyone what to do on the dance floor, and it feels horrible when you are on the receiving end.

3. The men who can dance OK and who will lull you into a false sense of security with the first tanda or two (perhaps spread over a few nights), and then start getting too close for comfort: lips almost on yours, groin where it should not be, or grasp not released between tangos. Alternatively, before the first tanda is over, they'll be inviting you for a 'coffee', asking for your phone number, or suggesting that you accompany them to another milonga later: not as serious as actually groping you, but very annoying nonetheless (see **Coffee invite**, **Serious offence** and **Unwanted attention** for tips about dealing with this type of behaviour).

The key to the success of all bottom feeders is that if they can, they make verbal invitations to you at your table, and when you've accepted once, it's awkward to refuse the next time.

What's the answer? Do not be pressured. Don't be so desperate to dance that you will accept anyone. Basically, follow **Rule 1: Only accept or invite a person you have observed dancing**, **Rule 2: Women — don't accept a verbal invitation unless you know the person or he is Pablo Veron** and **Rule 9: Know that you can say *No*** with a simple *No, gracias*, and all will be well. In the unfortunate instance that the man makes an unpleasant scene, just gently but firmly repeat the *No, gracias*, and he will eventually leave you alone.

Cabeceo

The cabeceo is the nod of the *cabeza* (head), combined with eye contact, used to secure a dance. Whether or not you use the cabeceo to make or accept invitations to dance in your home country, you must learn to do so in Buenos Aires, or you may never leave your seat in the more Traditional places. Maybe it doesn't come naturally to you to stare doggedly at prospective dance partners sitting far away on the other side of the room, but it will, *if you practise* from the day you arrive here. Once you've mastered the technique, you will not look back. I love the cabeceo because it avoids awkwardness between men and women who don't want to dance with each other, it's effective, and it gives both sexes a degree of power (differing degrees maybe, but power nonetheless).

Here's how it works.

Either from his seat, or from a standing position an unobtrusive distance away, the man will look at the woman he wishes to invite to dance, until she looks back at him. They catch eyes. Once he is sure she is holding his gaze, the man will invite the woman either with a nod, a sideways incline of the head, or a mouthed *Bailamos?* If she wants to accept, the woman will do so with a nod, and the contract has been made. The man will get up and walk until he is standing either in front of the woman's table or in a position as near as possible to it (and in some venues this might be the corner of the dance floor), and he will hold her eyes with his while he does so. The woman stays seated until the man reaches her and/or she is absolutely certain that she is the chosen one. Once there is no doubt, the woman stands and joins the man on the dance floor. The man may greet the woman with a word or two, or he may say nothing. The woman takes her cue from him and either returns the greeting or remains silent. She waits for him to offer her his embrace before moving towards him.

Tips for women:

1. Be bold. This is the key to success. Shrinking back into your seat and bashfully glancing at the crowds in the hope of a man looking your way WILL NOT DO! The behaviour is typical of new women in town and is born of a reluctance to stare at people and a lack of confidence, even terror. I look upon the cabeceo drill as a game requiring new skills, and a game I want to play to win. So I am determined and I have strategies. I muster all the magnetic energy at my command, I sit up straight and I look interested. If I have a man in my sights, I deliberately stare at him (that is, I give him the benefit of my most irrestistible mirada) until he notices me. I subtly move in my seat to attract his attention. If I don't have a particular guy in mind, I make a rapid scan of a row of men to see if any are looking at me. If one is, I complete my scan, in case someone even more desirable is looking at

me, and then I decide which gaze to return, or whether to return the gaze at all. I remember that I have power in the game: I can *will* guys to invite me with an intense and powerful mirada; I can choose who to accept; I can choose who to ignore. I am not a little wallflower, wilting in the shadow of the rows of sunflowers, hoping to be plucked out of pity; no, I always try to remember that I am a unique and beautiful sunflower and can seek out the sun myself. In the beginning it might be a case of following **Rule 11: Feel the fear, but dance anyway!** but you are going to have to be bold, or face the fact that you might be sitting on your butt for a very long time.

2.   Avoid too much vague scanning. A common mistake among newcomers is not to allow the gaze to rest for long enough. You need to let your eyes fix on your target and keep them there to indicate your interest.

3.   If you don't want to dance with someone, don't look at them, or look away and stay looking away when you see them looking at you.

4.   If a man is looking at you and you catch his eye, hold his gaze for a few seconds. If he doesn't make the invitation but just stares at you, or if he looks away, then you look away too for a second. Then look back. If he is still looking at you, hold his gaze again, and he will probably invite you. This game can go on a little while, with several glances away before the invitation. He is making sure you are truly interested. He doesn't want to invite you unless he is certain you will accept. In Buenos Aires, women do not nod first or make the invitation; the men do.

5.   To avoid embarrassment, wait until you see a clear invitation before smiling keenly or nodding. In fact it's probably better to avoid overt keenness altogether: cool tends to rule in Buenos Aires tango! In crowded venues there might be a bit of repeated nodding until both parties are certain that the deal has been done, even though more experienced dancers can achieve a successful cabeceo 'in one'.

6.   Once you think you have accepted an invitation, stay in your seat and keep your face pretty deadpan (however excited you may be) until the man is in front of you and you are absolutely certain it's you he wants. Milongas can be packed. It's sometimes easy to think that an invitation made to the woman sitting next to you or behind you, is for you. Don't find yourself standing on the dance floor without a

dance partner, a truly embarrassing moment that you can avoid easily just by waiting, bum fixed to seat, for the moment of certainty. On the other side of the equation, in your enthusiasm, do be careful not to intercept cabeceos or mistakenly steal dances that may have been intended for others.

7.   Once you have accepted an invitation to dance, try to keep your eyes on the man as he makes his way over, and avoid looking at any other men. Occasionally I have been faced with two men arriving at the table at the same time, both expecting to dance with me. I've managed to resolve this awkward situation by smiling a lot, apologising to the guy who got it wrong, and giving him a clear mirada at the start of the next tanda. If you've been part of a cabeceo cock-up of this nature, it's definitely best to apologise fast, even if you don't think the confusion was your fault; it's not great for a local guy to be stranded on the dance floor in front of other locals, and egos can be easily dented.

8.   In larger, more spacious venues, men (not women) are able to get up and move around the room to widen their cabeceo options. Be aware, therefore, that men may walk into or stand in your eye line and wait for you to look up and hold their gaze. If you're not interested, keep your eyes down or look away.

9.   Read the tips for men, below. Understand both sides of the deal so you can be more effective.

Tips for men:

1.   Relax. You have the power of invitation in Buenos Aires. You can choose who you want to invite. Enjoy that privilege.

2.   Be clear in your own mind about who you want to invite and make sure you communicate it to the woman you choose. Local men usually wait until they hear the music of the tanda, decide on the woman they wish to invite for that music, then fix their gaze on her. That's what local women will be expecting. Once you have decided on your target, turn your head towards her, let your eyes rest on her face and wait for her to look at you.

3.   Stare with intent, but avoid scary or over-the-top determined expressions. These are not necessary. You just need to let a relaxed

gaze rest on the woman, so that you can make eye contact with her if she allows it; you don't want to frighten her off.

4. If your target looks at you and makes eye contact, she is indicating her interest. She may glance away and then look back again: she's probably just making sure that you really are looking at *her*, because there could be other women seated all around. If she holds eye contact with you she is saying *If you invite me, I will accept.*

5. If your target looks away and doesn't look back, she is telling you that she isn't interested in dancing with you, for now at least. That's your cue to move your gaze to someone else.

6. If the front row of women won't look at you, look behind them: chances are the women seated further back will be less in demand than the front row, and might be keener to dance with an unknown.

7. Once you have achieved extended (a few seconds) eye contact with someone you wish to invite, give a deliberate (but not over-dramatic) nod of the head to make the invitation. There are alternatives to the nod. An incline of the head is a good example, and with time you will develop your own preferred cabeceo technique. A deliberate nod is a safe place to start because it's a clear invitation that even new-in-town tangueras will understand.

8. Don't stare at a woman if you don't intend to invite her. It's very confusing for women to make clear and prolonged eye contact with a man who then gives zero indication of an invitation. It happens, and I'm usually forced to think that he must be looking at the woman next to or behind me. On one such occasion, when I was able to speak to the man concerned afterwards, it turned out that he was a tango tourist and that he'd been staring at me and waiting for me to signal my interest with a nod or a gesture. Guys, sorry, but there won't be any such signal: the prolonged eye contact on my part *is* my signal and with it I state my intention to accept if I'm invited. In Buenos Aires the man makes the invitation with the nod and the woman returns it to accept and strike the deal to dance.

9. Once you are confident that you have achieved a successful cabeceo, try to maintain a degree of eye contact with your intended partner as you walk towards her. Your objective is to make sure that the woman you invited to dance is the woman who meets you on the dance floor. You can do this by keeping her in your sights until you

arrive to a position that is as close as possible to her table. She should then be in no doubt that you came to dance with her, and she will stand and walk towards you.

10. What happens if you've cabeceo-ed a woman, but as you move towards her table, another woman mistakenly stands up and steps into your path? You can ignore her and keep holding the gaze of the woman you have invited, and indeed this is what many Argentine men would do: yes, I know it's embarrassing for the woman who got it wrong, but she should have stayed in her seat until you were right in front of her table. Or, you can choose to dance with the woman you did not invite, and find some way to signal to the other that you are sorry (and in this case, it would be polite to invite her for the next tanda if at all possible).

11. What about if you've cabeceo-ed a woman, but by the time you arrive, or while you are on your way to her, she stands and starts dancing with someone else? Well, you just have to divert your course and find the most natural way to return to your seat, pop out to the restroom or the balcony, or chat to someone you know. Minimise the risk of awkward situations by being aware of what is going on around you. If a man sitting close to you gets up at exactly the same time as you, stay behind him and keep your eye on both the woman and him: thus if he arrives to her before you, you can divert your course and avoid the 'two men one woman on the dance floor' scenario.

12. Struggling to achieve successful cabeceos from your seat? In some venues (observe the local men to determine which ones) you can follow **Rule 6: Work the room** by moving to a standing position, either in an aisle or near the bar: this could widen your cabeceo options. However, avoid too much wandering around or you may be mistaken for a bottom feeder — it's a tricky balance!

13. If you have achieved your cabeceo from a standing position in an aisle, you will walk down it towards the woman's table and escort her on to the dance floor from there. The corners of the dance floor tend to be where many dancers enter the pista, but it's possible to step on to the floor anywhere. As you usher your partner out ahead of you, do be careful not to obstruct the moving dancers; wait for a gap.

14. Read the tips for women, above. Understand both sides of the deal so you can be more effective.

Tips for everyone:

1.   In some venues, where men and women are seated on opposite sides of the dance floor, it's necessary to perform your cabeceo fast at the start of a tanda, because once people start dancing, it can be extremely difficult to see past the moving bodies to the potential partners on the other side of the room.

2.   If you don't achieve a cabeceo in the first tango of a tanda, don't give up, because dancers will often invite strangers during the second or third, so as not to risk a whole tanda with an unknown quantity.

3.   The locals will wait to hear the music of the tanda before selecting a partner, and they will have favourite partners for *vals*, *milonga* (see **Non-tango tandas** for more information) or particular orchestras. They also might have a long list of regulars that they dance with every week (see **Regular or tourist?**), and their dance cards might already be overflowing. These are just a couple of reasons why they might not pick you. It isn't always about you, you see, so on those nights when you don't dance much (and they happen to us all), don't let your confidence bruise too easily.

Cameras

Use your camera with discretion. I do use mine in some venues, but I restrict myself to taking photos of friends at the table or shots of the dance floor from an appropriate distance. I prefer not to use a flash, as I think it may disturb others. In the Tourist-circuit venues it's far more acceptable to take random shots of the venue, the dance floor or the dancers, but in the Traditional venues you might offend people, because personal privacy is valued. My advice is to observe what others do, suss out the appropriate behaviour and follow suit. If you are a professional photographer and want to take more than a few holiday snaps, it would be courteous to request permission from the organiser.

If there is a tango exhibition at the milonga, it's usually fine to film or take photos. You'll see everyone get their cameras out, but do avoid using flash so as not to distract the performers.

Classes

See **Group classes**, **Private classes** and **Tango schools**.

Coat check

Many venues have a *guardarropa* (wardrobe or coat check where you can leave both clothes and bags), either at the entrance where you pay for your *entrada* or just inside. For a small fee, you exchange your stuff for a numbered ticket that you surrender as you leave in exchange for your stuff. Is it safe to leave valuables in your checked-in bags? I've never had any problems, and in some busy venues, where you might not have your own table, it'll surely be safer to leave your things in the guardarropa than stashed in a corner, mixed up with bags belonging to strangers.

In the most Traditional milongas, it's considered good form to leave big bags as well as coats, hats, scarves, gloves (I'm talking winter bulk here) at the coat check, before you cross the threshold of the milonga salón. In the high-powered places, you are on show and need to follow **Rule 5: Look the part** from the moment you arrive. Also, the seats can be packed in tight, there's no space for anything other than yourself, and you might end up elbowing someone as you try to extract yourself from your outdoor garments.

Códigos

The tango world of Buenos Aires functions the way it does because of its *códigos* (codes or etiquette), rooted in history and tested over decades. To me, they are the tango world's secrets and I have grown to respect them because they explain most of what I see in the milongas, and they tell me how to behave when I go out to dance. When we all know the codes, we all know where we are; we can fit in and avoid causing offence.

To foreigners, some of the códigos may seem strange and make us feel uncomfortable. At first, I wanted to change one or two of them myself, especially those concerning couples, as I walked on eggshells through love and tango in the early days of my relationship with my own Argentine, Carlos. But I've come to respect the fact that the Argentine culture is very different to my British one, and that it actually isn't my place to waltz in and expect things to be as I would like. When discovering the etiquette of the Buenos Aires milongas, I think it best to stick to **Rule 7: Leave your expectations behind**, and go with the flow instead. Plus, you do have some choice in the matter: how closely you will have to adhere to the most conservative códigos depends on where you choose to dance, and this may be a factor for you to consider when following **Rule 3: Seek out your 'tango homes'**. The codes are strictly adhered to in the most Traditional milongas, but have become diluted in some Tourist-circuit and Informal places. Having said that, I still think you can behave more confidently and appropriately, wherever you are, if you're aware of how things once were and still might be. In other words, you won't get caught out.

I wish I could give you a definitive list of the 'Top 100 BsAs milonga códigos you must know', but if I tried, I'm sure someone would tell me I'd missed out the most vital one. And it isn't easy to separate one from the other. However, here are some códigos that give you the basic knowledge required to enjoy the more Traditional places; they're arranged chronologically from the moment you arrive at the milonga:

- Pay your *entrada*, and if the coat check is at the entrance, leave bulky outdoor clothes there.
- On entry to the milonga, wait to be seated by the milonga host.
- Sit in the seat offered by the host, or politely ask for an alternative.
- If you sit as a couple, neither of you will be considered a potential dance partner by other dancers. The alternative is to sit separately, and even better, arrive separately (see **Couples** for details).
- Respect those seated around you. Be polite. Don't knowingly steal or move other people's seats. Try to avoid blocking the view of the dancers behind you.
- If invited to join a friend's table, let the friend select your seat.
- Women, change your shoes and/or clothes in the baños.

• Make and accept invitations to dance using the cabeceo, which has its own set of códigos (see **Cabeceo** for details). Men invite the women, not the other way around.

• Men, invite the 'available dancers' only: women who are sitting with a male partner are out of bounds, unless the man is seen to dance with others.

• Do dance. Don't perform. Show respect to other couples at all times. Keep your feet on the floor. Beware of sweeping your feet in wide circles. Keep your steps as small as you need to, in order not to interfere with other dancers.

• No talking while dancing. Boys, no running commentaries about the state of the floorcraft; no announcements to your partner on the subject of her dancing (for example, hissing *Hook* in her ear, when she chooses not to perform a led gancho because she believes it inappropriate for a packed pista); and no endless apologies for anything at all. Girls, no endless apologies either. Something goes awry on my part, I just keep quiet or maybe let out a soft chuckle to let my guy know I'm aware of my 'mistake'. I'm learning that the true gentlemen tangueros want me to feel beautiful at all times and actually prefer their own quests for tango bliss not to be punctuated by words like *Oops* or *Sorry*.

• Men, navigate the dance floor with the whole dancing population in mind: the more experienced men dance in the outer lane, the less experienced in the middle; there may be another lane in between the outer and the middle if the floor is large. Be considerate towards each other, keep moving with the whole body of dancers, and don't hold up the counter-clockwise flow of the *ronda* (the line of dance). Follow the line of dance. Don't cut across other dancers. Stay either in your lane or in the middle.

• Women, keep your eyes slightly open when the floor is crowded, so you can be aware of what's going on around you. However skilled your leader is, others will come so close that you'll want to consciously scale down your footwork to avoid injuries.

• If you do bump another couple, pause briefly and check they are OK, or at the very least, catch their eye or raise a hand to signal that you are sorry. If you get bumped by another couple, handle it calmly.

- Dance with your partner to the very end of a tanda (unless a serious offence occurs; for more details, see **Serious offence**).
- Between dances in a tanda, let go of your partner until the dancing begins again. You can chat in this interval or enjoy a companionable silence. The man offers the embrace when he is ready to resume dancing. Boys, if you're not sure when to set off again, see **Tanda** for the details.
- Men, if you want to match the most experienced Argentine dancers, you can attempt to finish the tanda right in front of the woman's table, thus delivering her home safely.
- Men, wherever you end the tanda, escort your partner back to her table. This is the mark of a gentleman. Show the local women that you are not just another ignoramus *turista* by performing this small courtesy. It's considered rude not to.
- Thank your partner at the end of a tanda with a *Gracias* or a *Muchas gracias*.
- Clear the floor during the cortina.
- Avoid dancing consecutive tandas with the same partner, as it can be seen as an indication of romantic interest. A maximum of three tandas, spaced throughout the night, should be fine (but in my own experience, two is safer). More and you could find yourself on dodgy ground.
- Men never invite themselves to sit at a woman's table.
- Pay for your food and drinks. If invited to join a friend's table, don't forget to settle up for your drinks before leaving.
- Tip the waiter. Tip the toilet attendant if you use the baños.
- If you do end up striking a deal on a coffee invite (see **Coffee invite** for the lowdown), expect to meet each other in the street outside the milonga rather than leave together.
- Thank the host or organiser and the DJ before you leave.

The key to understanding how and when to apply the códigos is observation, observation and observation. OK, and making a few mistakes is allowed too — God knows, I've made some. Take marching in to Canning with a friend and incurring the wrath of the host by choosing the best seats in the house the first time I ever went there (well, the table *was* empty!).

Coffee invite

When is an invitation to coffee not an invitation to coffee? Well, when it comes from a man to a woman in the milongas of Buenos Aires, of course. I will never forget the first time I told Carlos that I was meeting an English guy here for a coffee. It took me about twenty-four hours to convince him that we weren't going to be having sex, or at least having a conversation about it. This is a huge cultural difference between South America and Western Europe/North America. Maybe it isn't always the case, but just be aware that if you are a woman and you accept an invitation to meet a man outside the milonga for a 'coffee', you might find yourself standing outside a love hotel instead; at the very least, the guy will think you are very keen on him. For information on how to deal with unwanted coffee invites and indeed all other unwanted invites that might come your way in the milongas, see **Unwanted attention**. Then again, just in case you can't resist... **Love hotels** get their own entry too.

Cortina

After every tanda, the *cortina* (the Spanish word for curtain) music is played. It'll be something far removed from tango, so you can't really mistake it: pop, swing, salsa, rock 'n' roll... you name it, I've heard it in Buenos Aires. It's the signal for all dancers to clear the floor and return to their seats. It isn't the done thing to dance to the cortina music, though you might see a few enthusiastic couples strutting their stuff.

During the cortina, I like to decide whether I might dance the next tanda (if it turns out to be music I can't resist), and if so, who could be next in line for my mirada – especially important in venues where dancers on the floor can obscure my view of potential partners once the tanda starts. I can't decide finally until I hear the music, but I can consider my options. I'll already have an idea of whether I'm expecting tango, milonga or vals, and that will inform my thinking. Check out the entry **Non-tango tandas**, so that you too can start to calculate what might be coming next and be a tiny bit prepared.

Couples

If a man and woman enter a Traditional Buenos Aires milonga together and sit together at the same table, they are declaring that they are a couple and that they wish to dance only with each other. This is one of the milonga códigos. The whole idea can be a bit of a shock for visiting couples (and singles) who might be used to something else back home, but I'm afraid in Buenos Aires it's the way things are, so if you want to dance with other people as well as with your partner, you have to get creative.

Some couples who come to Buenos Aires solve the issue by going out separately and dancing in different milongas, but that tends to happen most when partners find out that their 'tango homes' don't coincide, and also when they are here for a while. If you're only visiting for a couple of weeks, the chances are that you'll want to spend at least some of your dancing time in the same room as your partner.

If the two of you want to attend a Traditional-style milonga (with traditional seating arrangements; see **Seating** for more information) and dance with others, your best option is to arrive separately and sit separately: you can still cabeceo each other, but also other dancers. This works: Carlos and I do it. It's great, because we can dance an early tanda together, so our dancing can be seen; however, we stagger our arrival times, because some men will not dance with a woman if they think she is with someone else.

Sitting separately has its downsides: you can't enjoy a meal, a drink or a chat with your partner, and you only get to talk to them in the breaks between dances in the tandas that you share. To avoid confusion or disappointments, you might need to work out in advance which tandas you want to dance together — in our case the vals, plus some of our favourite orchestras... Ah, now perhaps you begin to see the potential complexities.

In the Tourist-circuit and Informal places, the couple can sit together, but try a different strategy: the man can get up, leave the table, walk around the room and cabeceo others from a standing position; the woman is left alone at the table and other men might invite her, but only once they see her man dancing with someone else.

Occasionally, a tourist man who is unaware of the milonga códigos will approach a couple at their table and invite the woman in the couple to dance. If you are the couple, then how you handle it is up to you: if you are newbies yourselves, who hadn't realised that couples were out of bounds to other dancers, then maybe you'll find it a welcome intrusion of the 'Oh phew, someone is actually asking one of us to dance rather than ignoring us' variety. Personally, I would find it an *unwelcome* intrusion, because if I am sitting alone with my guy, I am declaring my desire to be left alone with him and it can feel awkward having to deliver a face-to-face refusal to a stranger.

If you're with a group of friends involving Argentine couples, it's polite to request the permission of the man to dance with the woman: you could say, *Permiso?* (Excuse me, may I?). I know that maybe it isn't very European or North American or, well, modern, but it is the Argentine tango way. I read a lovely explanation of this somewhere, which said that it isn't that the woman is the property of the man, but that by asking permission openly, you are letting the couple know that you will respect their relationship: I like that idea.

There are some milongas at the weekend that are great for couples and groups of friends who want to dance just with each other. There are no rows of traditional seating for solo dancers. One of my favourite milongas for this is La Baldosa on a Friday night. You can have a good dinner and enjoy dancing on the large floor made of *baldosa* (paving stone/hard tile). There is very often an excellent exhibition and, on special occasions, a live orchestra. Club Sunderland, on a Saturday night, is very popular with couples and groups, and in the quieter seasons has an especially local vibe.

Traditionally, Saturday night is couples' night out in Tangoland Buenos Aires. On Saturdays solo dancers seeking Traditional-style tango must head to the milongas known to welcome solo dancers, or risk disappointment: early evening, La Milonga de Los Consagrados in La Leonesa is a good option, and later, the milongas in El Beso and La Nacional, and Cachirulo in Club Villa Malcolm are three possibilities.

The huge upside of being in a 'tango couple' in Buenos Aires is that you can visit any práctica or milonga of whatever type, sit together, eat together, dance together and enjoy the overall vibe of the place, without feeling lonely; if you're in a couple and happy just to dance with each other, then the pressure is off — you can relax and enjoy the shared experience, as many Argentines do.

Crowds

It's no good complaining: the dance floors of Buenos Aires get crowded.

The Tourist-circuit venues especially can be absolutely packed: on their most popular nights, when they have a live orchestra playing, when a famous couple is performing an exhibition, when there is a tango festival, if there is a *feriado* (bank holiday) the following day, and in the high season.

Some people like the buzz of full venues: Salón Canning, when it's so chocker that there is barely room to stand in the aisles, can be quite a heady experience and can elicit delighted internal cries of *Bloody hell, I'm here in the world capital of tango!* Some people relish the challenge of dancing in a tiny space, and as a woman I can derive great pleasure from the closest of embraces and the teensiest of musical steps (if I feel safe in the guy's arms). On the other hand, by the time you've been bumped or spiked by someone's four-inch heel a zillion times in one tanda, the shine can start to rub off. Then you might start longing for quieter moments on the dance floor. Here are my ideas for finding them:

•   Come to Buenos Aires in the quieter months for tango tourists (usually June, September and January), or at least outside of the main festival dates. See **tangobuenosaires.gob.ar** for the latest on the annual *Tango Festival y Mundial* (Tango Festival and World Tango Championship).
•   In busier periods, avoid the Tourist-circuit venues, and head further afield, although sometimes it seems that wherever you go there are crowds.
•   The final hour of any milonga is quieter than the peak hours. The masses tend to head home after the dance exhibition or live orchestra

performance, and then there is more space to dance. Beat the crush with the first part of **Rule 10: Stay late**. The earliest hour of the milonga is always spacious too and is good for being seen before the place gets too packed.

Dance floors

The *pistas* (dance floors) of Buenos Aires are for dancing and for brief chats with your partner between dances. They are not for short cuts to get to the other side, for teaching your partner new steps, or for walking all over in pursuit of good photographs. Men who have achieved a successful cabeceo should walk around the edge of the floor to get to the woman. The exception is at the start of the tanda when the floor is empty, but once dancing has begun in earnest, don't be tempted to play dodgems with the dancing couples.

The floors are usually made of *madera* (wood, and easier on the feet) or *baldosa* (stone or tile, and harder on the feet, and sometimes becoming slightly damp and tacky as the evening progresses). I need to wear different soles depending on the dance floor: slippery and I use rubber; sticky and I use leather; and for in-between conditions, I use tough suede. Men could try 2x4alpie shoes (see **10 Tango Shoe Stores** in **Appendix B**), which have interchangeable soles in their unique system: one shoe, three soles, and you could use them all — sometimes in one night. If you don't have interchangeable soles, then water underfoot can stop slips, and talcum powder can stop stickiness. In summer when stone floors get damp with humidity as the night wears on, hosts may put talc (or something like it) down at the corners of the dance floor so you can coat the soles of your shoes. But don't overdo it!

I confess I'm not a floor expert, so in *Happy Tango* I distinguish only between wooden floors and hard-tile floors, where wood means wood of any and every kind, and hard-tile means everything else (stone, marble, ceramic, whatever...). I do point out any floors that I've noticed to be particularly tricky or extra fabulous, but that's as detailed as it gets. If you like dancing on wood, you'll find some of the city's smoother examples in Salón Canning, Centro Región Leonesa, El Beso and La Nacional.

Club Gricel has a sprung pine floor loved by many, but it's ageing and slightly rough underfoot in places.

Disappointment

I've had plenty of disappointments on my tango journey since the day I first arrived in Buenos Aires.

I thought all Argentines would be fantastic dancers and they weren't. I hoped the most popular milongueros would pick me — they didn't. I wanted my teacher to tell me I had the potential to be a great dancer the first time he led me around the room, but instead he had me walk up and down decorating my steps, and I tipped and wobbled in front of him. **Rule 7: Leave your expectations behind** was born of moments like these. I now believe that the fastest way to put a smile on my face in a tango salón or a tango class is to leave the fantasies at home and be prepared to embrace reality instead. But it's not always easy. However much I try to guard against it, the occasional disappointing experience will still be mine. Perhaps 'disaster' strikes on a night when my magnetic energy is low but I decide to head out to the milonga anyway, or when I make a poor judgement regarding a dance partner and want to kick myself afterwards, or when I sit and feel ill at ease and invisible in a place that really isn't my cup of tea. Situations like these might spark a bit of a moan, a complaining rant, a few hours of self pity, a minor panic accompanied by a question like *What the hell am I doing here?* or even some tears. I've certainly cried over tango in Buenos Aires and I don't think I've ever met a tango tourist here who wouldn't understand why I have: it can seem a tough scene to crack at times, and it can sure play havoc with our egos, our confidence and our self-belief.

However, I do believe in living in the solution and not the problem, and so I am constantly seeking ways to minimise my unhappy experiences and make joy mine instead. The Rules are the direct result of my own quest for bliss. They are my shield against many of the grim situations that can cause disappointment to flood in. And I know that if you use them in conjunction with all the other knowledge in this book, they can be effective for you too.

Dress for success

Now we are really talking **Rule 5: Look the part**. With clothes that are comfortable, fabulous and you, you'll ramp up your self-confidence for following **Rule 4: Exude magnetic energy**.

The more Traditional the place, the more dressy the glad rags; the more Informal it is, the more hip and trendy the gear. Wherever you are, touches of elegance and glamour never go amiss. Two of my best outfits for reliably getting dances are:

- A strapless, black-satin dress with an above-the-knee hemline — it's classy, shows off my legs and catches the light when I dance.

- A low-waisted, figure-hugging skirt combined with a halterneck top and, dare I say it, an inch of taut tummy-flesh (on my slimmer days) revealed between the two.

I can't help wondering if these little ensembles work for me just because I love myself in them and they give my magnetic energy a boost. That could be it, and so despite all the tips coming up, to be comfy, relaxed and 100% *yourself* in what you're wearing is probably what counts above all else in the quest to attract the dancers that are right for *you*.

Tips for women:

1.   The men of Buenos Aires like their partners to look feminine and elegant. I've heard it said that some men in the more Traditional places prefer to dance with women who are wearing skirts or dresses... Even in the scruffier and more Informal places such as La Viruta, if you're an unknown female you'll be more likely to be invited onto the floor if you look classy: grungy jeans and a sloppy T-shirt are unlikely to do it for most people.

2.   Wearing a colour, or at least a splash of colour, can help a woman to stand out in the rows of women at a milonga: all black can leave you merging into the shadows. However, some men argue that the best dancers tend to wear all black. You'll have to decide on your strategy.

3.   Remember that you are seen from the back when dancing. Back-less dresses or tops can look fabulous, if you have the body to carry

them off in style, and skirts with detail on the back attract attention. So does anything that emphasises the curves of your bum. I can't help noticing that the favourite garb of many is a G-string/thong under some kind of smooth material in trousers or a dress (yes, you did read that right — I think they choose the G-string first and then show its presence off with a clingy fabric). You will have to decide if you want to buy into all that (and 'that' includes cleavage or any bit of flesh on show too). I'm telling you, it will get you dances. But, on the flip side, you don't want to attract the wrong types, so beware of taking it too far.

4.   Make sure your outfit is going to stay where you want it. Mini skirts can rise and become micro, and the closest of embraces can play havoc with tops that are not well anchored. You could find yourself revealing more than you'd planned. If you've got to keep thinking about it and pulling it down, round or up, it's going to affect your dancing.

5.   Some Argentine men wear suit jackets with buttons. Don't wear something that catches easily. Avoid belts with buckles as they can lock onto the guys' belts. And no jewellery that might scratch the men's clothes either.

6.   Choose clothes in fabrics that are pleasant to touch: some say that satin and silk are much loved by the gents.

7.   When it's hot, take a Japanese-style folding fan to cool you between tandas, and tissues to wipe your brow (many men's heads, as well as their bodies, perspire profusely). Avoid single-coloured fabrics that might show patches of sweat: either yours or his. I will never forget the time I stood back from a guy and found a huge damp patch on the front of my dress from his soaking shirt. *Ugh!* La Ideal is one of the worst venues for heat, as there is no air conditioning and the ceiling fans are inadequate. Niño Bien in Centro Región Leonesa can also be bad, as the air conditioning isn't always up to dealing with the crowds.

8.   Air conditioning and/or winter can make some venues very chilly, so take layers. But do be warned that cold can do terrible things to your magnetic energy: just watch that you don't end up wrapping yourself in a shawl and shrinking back into your seat. I've sat next to women doing this and it really stops the invitations coming. By all means throw your shawl over your shoulders, but try to stay looking

open and interested: no folded arms, no rounded backs, and no actually disappearing into the shawl. Oh hell, I've done it myself a few times — that's how I know.

9. You want to be remembered from one visit to a milonga to another, so don't be tempted to wear a different wig every night, and, without going over the top, do create your own unique and memorable signatures. I've got red-framed spectacles and I know they help to get me noticed, plus I often use large pink-flower clips to keep my hair from falling into the guy's face. Both these details help men to remember me.

10. Think about the impression your tango shoes give to local dancers. I've heard on the grapevine that flashy new shoes can put off the more serious tangueros because it's obvious that the shoes haven't been worn in. Designer bling might be shouting *I'm a rich tourist on holiday*, and that could attract a different type of guy entirely. I tone down my tango shoe glitz for the more local milongas, as I feel more comfortable fitting in than standing out... I will wear a designer brand, but I'll pick one that's well worn and obviously seen a bit of action.

Tips for men:

1. Local men make an effort when they go out to dance, particularly in the Traditional and Tourist-circuit places. Even in more Informal venues, many men dress on the smart side. Care with clothes may mean care both on the dance floor and in life: anyway, it impresses me. Jackets, ironed shirts, trousers other than jeans, groomed hair, and a touch of cologne are the norm in Buenos Aires Traditional tango, and even in other places, they will get you noticed.

2. Some tango venues can get very hot in summer. Take a spare shirt or shirts if you think you might need to change — please don't get so sweaty that you leave patches of damp o⌐ ⌐or a close embrace. It's a good idea to make the fr colour to the first one, so that the women noti⌐ smelling sweet. Have a clean handkerchief in your brow between tangos if necessary, and i onto the side of your partner's face, offer tⅼ

first: I've been really grateful for that thoughtfulness a few times. You can always take a break outside too, if you need to cool down.

3.   Make sure suits and shirts are of fabrics that are pleasant to the touch in a close embrace, especially in hot weather: natural feels better than synthetic to a woman wrapped tight in a man's arms.

4.   Signatures are good for men as well as for women. I find it really hard to remember faces after one tanda, even if the tanda was good. Make it easy for me with a striking suit, a key chain, wide trousers, slicked-back hair, noticeable tango shoes... oh anything that reminds me that the fabulous middle-height, middle-aged, brown-haired, brown-eyed guy that I met in the half-darkness in El Beso last week was you.

And three tips for everyone:

1.   In certain milongas, such as Cachirulo, jeans are frowned upon and you might not be allowed in. In many other places, jeans are acceptable, but if in doubt, don't wear them the first time you visit. Check the place out and then decide for next time.

2.   To fit in, steer clear of the stereotypical stage tango gear. You'll rapidly spot that most women avoid dresses split to the crotch, fishnet stockings with thigh tops on show, and roses between their teeth. As for hats on the dance floor... Argentine men don't do them.

3.   It may seem obvious to most people, but don't even think about going to the milonga without showering first. A splash of perfume doesn't hide much in close embrace. Too much perfume or aftershave is equally repellent. Deodorant that can cope with the Buenos Aires summers, and minty fresh breath are good. Garlic, raw onions, fish and salami can't be disguised by even the most aggressive of mouthwash products, so save these stinky foods for early morning snacks after the milonga, rather than indulging in them beforehand.

Before arriving in Argentina, I imagined that Buenos Aires would be full of shops selling 'tango clothes'. I quickly realised that most Argentine (non-professional) tango dancers just buy ordinary clothes that are le for tango, and that the shops selling clothes especially made for tango tend to be frequented mainly by tourists. Here are five tango clothes retailers, in case you want to check them out:

Tango Imagen (**tango-imagen.com**) at Anchorena 606
Tangomoda (Facebook **Tango Moda**) at Balcarce 961, 1st floor, Depto 4
Mimi Pinzon (**mimipinzon.com.ar**) at Venezuela 3502
Asignatura Pendiente (**asignaturatangovip.com.ar**) by appointment
Devora M. (**etsy.com/shop/devoram** and **info@devoram.com**): a range of versatile clothes that cross over easily between times on and off the dance floor; online shop or in Buenos Aires by appointment.

And, especially for the boys, there is a fascinating tailor that offers to run up *trajes* (suits) and *sacos* (jackets) for tango dancers, at Pueyrredón 367, in the rather manic shopping district of Once. Its name, *El Rey de los Pantalones* (The King of Trousers, to be found online at **reydelpantalon.com.ar**), originally got me through the door to investigate, though I've not actually sampled the products myself.

If you opt to stick with the locals and buy ordinary clothes that could be suitable for tango, the Once district is actually a very good place to start, though it is a case of pile it high, sell it fairly cheap and don't expect it to last too long. Begin at Pueyrredón and Corrientes, and once you've explored the craziness of Pueyrredón in the direction of Avenida Rivadavia, walk down Corrientes towards the Obelisco; there are several *galerías* (covered arcades) on the right-hand side and they have many small stores offering a wide range of fashions.

If you want more refined and more expensive clothes shopping, you could try Galerías Pacífico (**www.galeriaspacifico.com.ar**) on the corner of Florida and Córdoba in the Microcentro. Another famous mall is Abasto Shopping (**www.abasto-shopping.com.ar**) at Corrientes 3247 in Abasto, and you could combine it with a trip to pay homage to Carlos Gardel: visit the Museo Carlos Gardel at Juan Jaurés 735 and take a look at his statue in Pasaje Carlos Gardel between Jean Jaurés and Anchorena. There are a few tango shoe and clothes shops on Anchorena (including Tango Imagen, who make clothes to order, as well as selling off the shelf), so you could check those out too.

Entrada

The *entrada* (entry fee) is paid on the way in. In exchange for your money, you are usually given a ticket, which you show to the milonga host when you enter the salón: unless they take it from you, hang on to it because later there may be a *sorteo* (draw or raffle) of the entry ticket numbers. Afternoon/early-evening milongas generally come cheaper than night-time milongas. The most famous Tourist-circuit venues can have the highest entry prices, and the amount can go up if there is a live orchestra playing. Occasionally, if you arrive extremely late for a milonga, the entry fee is waived. A few places have a cheaper ticket price for early birds, print two-for-one vouchers, or even charge women a little less than men. These sorts of offers tend to vary, so I'll leave you to discover the latest bargains for yourselves.

Exhibitions

In many of the Tourist-circuit milongas, there will be an exhibition by professional dancers at some point during the night. A couple may dance a set of two or three tangos, milongas or valses. Sometimes more than one couple will dance. Occasionally the performance may be folk dancing or another non-tango style. The performance is often not until 1.30 or 2am, at the late-night milongas. If a live orchestra is playing, the dance exhibition will usually be in the middle of the live music set. Don't be tempted to talk loudly throughout the show, even if you aren't enjoying it much, because many other people will want to watch and listen.

How can you find out who's performing when and where?

- Visit the websites of the venues/milongas/prácticas: some organisers, like Parakultural, in the case of Salón Canning, and La Viruta, publish their shows for the month ahead (see **20 Places to Try First** in **Part 3** for links to the major websites).
- Check the websites or the paper copies of the free Buenos Aires tango magazines that come out early in each month (see **The Listings** in **Part 3** for the links).
- Pick up flyers handed out at the milongas.

Now it's confession time. A long time ago on a Saturday night in Club Sunderland, a vals started to play and Carlos grabbed my hand and pulled me to my feet. Within seconds we were dancing. Within a few more seconds we'd sat down again and Carlos had pulled his jacket up over his head, and there he stayed for a very long time. I had no jacket with which to cover my face and I glowed red with embarrassment. We'd been so busy chatting to our friends that we'd both completely missed the fact that the exhibition had started... Oh my God! Occasionally some disaster like this happens to everyone, but ouch.

Famous

Do you love watching the professionals on YouTube? Are you sometimes tempted to carry an autograph book to tango festivals? If so, you will love spotting the famous faces of tango in Buenos Aires. Some like to hang out in the Tourist-circuit milongas at front-row tables with their mates and buckets of champers, others slip into La Viruta for a few tandas with their friends at 4am, and yet more pop up in the most Traditional places and keep a fairly low profile.

Can you approach them and say how much you admire them? Occasionally I do, if they have just performed an exhibition and I've really loved it: I think it can be nice to say thanks and tell them how much they have inspired me — assuming they have, of course. Friends of mine have taken the same opportunity, and asked about the possibility of private tango classes. We've kept it brief and it's gone down just fine.

If the famous are not performing an exhibition and are out with their friends, I'd probably leave them to their evening and a bit of privacy.

Food and drink

Most venues sell a basic range of drinks: from champagne and wines to *gaseosas* (fizzy drinks) and bottled water. Coffee is usually available too, but it's only worth sampling if it comes from a coffee machine. Don't expect to be able to order cocktails or anything other than the most basic spirits: vodka, gin and whisky might be options, but not necessarily in brands familiar to foreigners.

Many places offer snack food (see *empanadas* and *picada* in the list of foods below), and in some venues it's possible to order a more substantial meal: on the Informal circuit, La Viruta offers decent food (earlier on in the night), La Catedral does good vegetarian dishes, and Club Villa Malcolm serves up a great range of simple meals; Club Sunderland, La Baldosa and Sueño Porteño (where there is a separate restaurant) are popular places for Argentines to enjoy dinner with their dancing; and at the most Traditional end of the spectrum, even El Beso has been known to offer a pretty full menu, but whether you really want to tuck into a main course when you are trying to attract the attention of some of the most popular dancers in Buenos Aires, only you can decide. Wherever you are, if you're hungry, ask for the menu, *La carta, por favor*. Prices are usually reasonable. You have to pay cash. In most milongas, there is waiter service.

Here are a few of the most basic milonga food and drink options, so that you know what to ask for:

agua sin gas / *agua con gas* — still water / sparkling water

gaseosas — fizzy drinks (and the usual international brands are available)

copa / *botella de vino* — glass / bottle of wine (*tinto* is red, *blanco* is white)

cerveza — beer (it will probably be a bottle and could be quite large)

botella de champán — bottle of champagne (sometimes offered in different sizes, and also available by the glass)

café sólo / *café con leche* / *cortado* — small black coffee / large milky coffee / small coffee with dash of milk

empanadas de carne / *pollo* / *jamón y queso* — mini pasties filled with minced beef / chicken / ham and cheese (if vegetarian empanadas are available, they are likely to be *cebolla y queso* or *verdura* — cheese and onion or spinach or chard)

picada — a plate of assorted cold meat, cheese, olives and potato chips

manís (or sometimes *maní* or *maníes*) — peanuts

papas fritas — crisps/potato chips (can also mean hot chips or French fries, but not usually in the milongas)

It's not on to take your own food and drink. A discrete square of chocolate you can probably get away with, but don't pull bottles of water or sandwiches out of your bag... unless you're at La Glorieta, which is outside and where no refreshments are for sale.

Don't forget to pay your bill for drinks and food before you leave. It can be very easy to forget and just walk out, and the *mozos* (waiters) end up paying unpaid bills out of their own pockets. Each waiter usually covers a certain area of the room. If necessary track him or her down at the bar. Before the waiters get to know you, they might expect you to pay for your drinks and food when they deliver them to the table. Once they know your face, they're more likely to let you settle up at the end of the night. And don't be surprised to see the same waiters in several different milongas, because they tend to work a circuit of venues.

To ask for the bill, say *La cuenta, por favor.*

Give a tip of around 10% when you settle up. The mozos work hard and it's good to make friends, to ensure great service next time.

Gay-friendly tango

Want to dance same-sex tango or swap tango roles? Want a gay-friendly tango experience? Choose one of the two most famous Buenos Aires gay-friendly milonga scenes: La Marshàll milonga at El Beso on Friday night (with a práctica at Aires Tangueros, Rivadavia 1392, on Sunday night), and Tango Queer at Buenos Ayres Club on Tuesday night.

These milongas are Informal and open-minded in character. Tango Queer perhaps has the more Informal and relaxed atmosphere of the two, because of its San Telmo-style venue: bohemian with low lighting and an old, slightly rough wooden floor. La Marshàll in El Beso offers a smarter salón with a smooth wooden pista, in a famous venue that hosts several very Traditional milongas on other nights of the week; the Aires Tangueros venue is more laid-back in style. Tango Queer and La Marshàll each have a unique vibe, and my advice is to check them both out in the quest to follow **Rule 3: Seek out your 'tango homes'.**

Both Tango Queer and La Marshàll welcome everyone whether gay or not, and it's understood and accepted that if you go to either of these places you will see men dancing with men and women dancing with women. You might be asked to dance by someone of the same sex, and you can ask too: you can invite verbally and explain which role (the terms leader and follower are used) you'd like to dance, as not everyone dances both roles; you might also be asked to dance by someone of the opposite sex, as these places are popular with groups of friends and people who just want to dance in a relaxed, open-minded atmosphere.

If you want to get into this tango scene, it would be a great plan to take the group classes before the milongas and meet a few people to dance with afterwards. Alternatively, go with friends. The classes are, of course, gay-friendly, but they are popular with all dancers who want to learn to dance both tango roles. Once you get to know a few people, you will fast find out where else it's acceptable to dance same-sex tango in Buenos Aires. To be honest, in the Traditional and the more formal of the Tourist-circuit places it isn't, and even in some of the Informal places it isn't much seen.

La Marshàll (**lamarshallmilonga.com.ar** or Facebook **La MarSHàlL**) and Tango Queer (**tangoqueer.com** or Facebook **Tango Queer Buenos Aires**) are two places where you absolutely can do your thing in tango, free from restrictions or discrimination, even if it isn't the traditional Buenos Aires tango thing, and that's pretty cool I reckon.

Group classes

See also **Private classes**.

There are group classes running all day, every day, in most corners of the city, whether at tango schools or before the milongas and prácticas, and many are taught by the famous. You might base your choice of class on the teachers, the style of tango being taught, the reputation of a particular school or even the fact that you want to go to the milonga or práctica after the class.

Here are three options for seeking out group tango classes:

1.   Try a tango school (see **10 Tango Schools** in **Appendix A** for details of schools that my friends have enjoyed). Tango schools sometimes offer prácticas where you can practise with other students.
2.   Scan the listings of classes in the Buenos Aires tango magazines and on the websites of the individual tango venues, milongas and prácticas to see which places have classes running beforehand and who is teaching them (see **The Listings** in **Part 3** for the online links).
3.   Scour the advertisements in the tango magazines, as well as the listings, because tango schools, teachers, venues, milongas, prácticas and organisers of one-off seminars or festivals post their class details there.

There are advantages and disadvantages to group classes:

Advantages:

•   You'll meet like-minded people to dance with at the milongas.
•   The range of options can keep you interested from dawn until dusk: *técnica para mujeres* (women's technique), *técnica para hombres* (men's technique), body conditioning, yoga to assist your dancing, pilates to assist your dancing, milonga, vals, tango milonguero, tango salón, tango nuevo, canyengue, chacarera, zamba...
•   It's a cheap way to be taught by the famous. A private class with a Tango God might be well over a hundred dollars, whereas a group class with the same Tango God might cost fifty pesos. Discounts are often offered if you pay in advance for a block of lessons.

- It's a useful way to find a teacher for private classes.
- If the number of students is small, you might receive a high level of personal tuition at a rock-bottom price.
- If the group class is directly before a milonga, it can be a smooth transition between class and milonga. You'll be there with a few people from the class, you might get a reasonable seat, and you won't have to walk in alone once the milonga has begun.
- It can be fun!

Disadvantages:

- There can be a large number of students in the class, resulting in very little, if any, personal attention.
- There might be students who are not at a high enough dance level for the class, and you could find yourself partnered with one (hopefully you won't be one, and if you are in any doubt, you could always ask the teacher to help you decide).
- There can be a gender imbalance and not all classes involve partner rotation, so if possible, take your own partner.
- In some cases, when a sequence of moves is being taught, teaching can be mostly directed at the leaders, so followers might not feel they are getting value for money.
- Classes can be long: girls, you might want to have some flat dance shoes in your bag, in case the going gets a bit painful, especially if the class is before a milonga and you want to save your feet for the real thing.
- Many group classes can be entirely in Spanish. If you need it, find out if English is spoken before you decide whether to take the class.

Hosts and organisers

After you've paid to get into a milonga and received your entry ticket, you must wait (except in the more informal places) to be greeted and seated by the host. The host(s) might be the organiser(s) — the person or couple who runs a particular milonga. The organiser often makes an announcement at some point during the evening: birthdays, events, introduction to the show and so on. The host might (in some cases) be the organiser's assistant.

However empty the place looks when you enter, don't march in and choose the best seat available. You won't make any friends that way, and you'll be asked to move. Wait at the entrance for the host to approach you, give your name if you made a reservation, or explain that you don't have one, and wait to be seated. If you don't like the table you're offered, there may be a chance to ask for an alternative (if your Castellano is up to it), but politeness is essential: you want the milonga host on your side...

If you are serious about dancing in the most Traditional milongas, you'll tend to have a better chance of a decent seat if you turn up alone. The host will establish if you are on your own and, if you're lucky, will try to squeeze you in somewhere good.

When you leave, it's good form to thank the host. Maybe you'll be going back the next week. Milonga hosts do remember faces and names, and reward loyalty and good dancing with better seats on return visits.

Castellano you might need:

Buenas noches. Tengo una reserva. Mi nombre es... — Good evening. I have a reservation. My name is...

No tengo una reserva, pero estoy solo(a) — I don't have a reservation, but I am alone.

Somos una pareja / dos personas / cuatro personas — We are a couple / two people / four people.

Estás solo / sola? Sí, estoy solo / sola — Are you alone? Yes, I'm alone.

Knowledge matters

Among the thousands who dance in Buenos Aires on any given night, with all their different nationalities, dancing styles and skill levels, I think there are, broadly speaking, three groups of dancers: the Well-known, the Knowing and the Unknowing.

The Well-known

The best milongueros/teachers/professionals are the Well-known. The Buenos Aires tango scene is their territory: they have many friends and favourite dance partners; they have their regular places to dance; they will always be seated at the best tables; they understand all the traditions and códigos of the milongas. They can choose from the most favoured dancers in the room and they know that the remainder of the milonga population would love the chance of a dance with them. The Well-known will rarely dance with folk they do not recognise, unless they fancy them like crazy, think they can get them into bed, or want to persuade them to take a class. These people need to be sure that they look good when they dance: they are unlikely to risk an unknown quantity.

The Well-known also include the recognisable regulars who are thought of as desirable dance partners by other regulars. They may not be famous, but they dance socially in the same milongas every week and will have their favourite dance partners in those places. However, they'll be more flexible than the famous and will perhaps try a tanda or two with someone they haven't danced with before. They will be watching for potential partners who can dance and who clearly understand the codes of the milonga: they may possibly dance with an unfamiliar person who is clearly at their level and who is in the group of dancers that I refer to as the Knowing.

The Knowing

The people in this group dance well, know how to behave, and respect the traditions and códigos. They might have to work harder than the Well-known, but they will have access to a wide range of dance partners, because they often make up the majority of the dancing population. People in this group may not recognise each other's faces, but they do recognise each other by behaviour. This is the group I am in. After a few years of Buenos Aires tango, I can make decent judgements about who I want to dance with, just by watching: embrace, style and technique; body shape and height; energy and behaviour — all can influence my decision making. Dancers in this group observe potential partners both on and off the floor before making or accepting an invitation, and they miss nothing. Once again, it's true that appearance and physical attraction matter and can cause all rules to be broken: if someone in this group can't resist your looks or the intriguing energy that radiates from you, they may drop all their other usual criteria and dance with you, even if you are in the group I refer to as the Unknowing — this is life, not just tango.

The Unknowing

These are the people like me when I arrived in Buenos Aires: fresh-off-the-plane tango tourists, from beginners to improvers and beyond, coming from tango cultures far, far removed. I know now that I looked new in town, behaved new in town, attracted the bottom feeders who saw immediately that I was new in town... and virtually no-one else. It was a while before I worked out how to behave and fit in. Once I did, I began to avoid the pitfalls, danced more, smiled more and was happier in my Buenos Aires tango.

By reading this book, you are already on the journey of passing from the Unknowing to the Knowing. You can improve your chances of finding Happy Tango from day one, by following **Rule 5: Look the part**, behaving as if you belong, and gaining enough respect from the locals and regulars to up your prospects of dancing with them.

Live orchestras

It's fabulous to be able to dance to live tango orchestras. I always feel it gives me a glimpse into what tango may have been like once, long ago. Yes, the milongas get crowded on performance nights, but if you get the chance to dance to live tango music, then I don't think you should miss it. The larger Tourist-circuit venues such as Salón Canning, Confitería Ideal and La Viruta regularly host orchestras and smaller bands. Other venues also do, and if you are lucky enough to catch one of the more famous orchestras playing off the well-beaten track, the experience can be even more special.

Some popular tango orchestras you're likely to see here include Color Tango (**colortango.com.ar**), Los Reyes del Tango and Sexteto Milonguero (**sextetomilonguero.com.ar**).

La Viruta also offers regular live performances of electronic tango, with Otros Aires (**otrosaires.com**), Narcotango (**carloslibedinsky.com**) and Tanghetto (**tanghetto.com**) all featuring in the past. Maldita Milonga hosts Orquesta Típica El Afronte (**elafronte.com.ar**) every week.

How can you find out who's performing when and where?

- See the websites of the milongas: some organisers, like Parakultural (in the case of Salón Canning) and La Viruta, publish their shows for the month ahead (see **20 Places to Try First** in **Part 3** for links to the major websites).
- Check the websites or the paper copies of the free Buenos Aires tango magazines that come out early in each month (see **The Listings** in **Part 3** for the links).
- Pick up flyers handed out at the milongas.

Outside of the milongas there are wonderful opportunities to enjoy live orchestras all over the city. Here are three completely different ideas for tracking them down:

1. Keep an eye on the official **festivales.gob.ar** website. It links to details of the city's festivals, including the summer programme of concerts, outdoor milongas and tango exhibitions. In 2012, the programme ran throughout most of January and February and was called 'Verano en la Ciudad'. I was lucky enough to see the marvellous and inspiring *Café de los Maestros* (the 2008 film directed by Miguel Kohan) maestros play live as part of this programme, in 2009. A separate festival, the annual Tango Festival (see **tangobuenosaires.gob.ar**), also includes free concerts. In recent years the festival has been held in August, and the process for obtaining tickets is usually posted on the website; some concerts don't require tickets and you can just turn up on the day.

2. Visit the outdoor markets: Defensa street in San Telmo is stage to a number of tango orchestras on Sunday. Three days after I arrived in Buenos Aires, I saw an orchestra play there and remember being delighted by my very first sight of a line up of energetic *bandoneonistas*: it's now evolved into Orquesta Típica Misteriosa Buenos Aires (**misteriosabuenosaires.net**) and tours worldwide, as well as playing in city venues famous for hosting tango orchestras, such as Centro Cultural Torquato Tasso (**torquatotasso.com.ar**) at Defensa 1575 in San Telmo. For live folk music head to Feria de Mataderos (see **See** in **Part 4** for further details).

- 3. For a high-energy funky tango orchestra, try the exciting and popular Orquesta Típica Fernández Fierro (**fernandezfierro.com**). It plays at CAFF (**caff.com.ar** for the dates, and how to get tickets in advance), Sánchez de Bustamante 764 in Abasto, when not on tour or vacation. Get there early if you want a seat.

Love hotels

Also referred to as *hoteles de alojamiento, albergues transitorios* or *telos*, it's good to know love hotels exist, even if you don't make use of them, because you might hear whispers, and wonder.

Love hotels have delightful names like Dallas, *Sueños* (Dreams), and *Tu y Yo* (You and I), and rent their rooms by three-hour or five-hour turns to those in need of a place to take their lover, at whatever time of day or night. On busy nights (at weekends), there may be queues in reception. On slack nights (weekdays), you can snag a deal to take you right through until morning. They range from the dingy and basic (untried by me), to the upmarket and flashy (OK, I admit it, I've tried a couple). At the top end, they have themed rooms, love sofas, hydro-massage tubs (probably not to be recommended for health reasons) and all manner of sex toys for sale from the room service menu. Room service is usually via a special compartment in the room door, to preserve your privacy!

I think it's important to understand that love hotels are not just seedy. They are used by many perfectly respectable Argentines who live with their parents and need a private space, who want to escape the ears of their children, or who want to celebrate a special anniversary with a bit of spice. Of course, they're also used by prostitutes and their punters, by couples conducting secret affairs, and maybe even by you after you've just danced three consecutive tandas...

In daylight, you can spot a love hotel by the small *Albergue Transitorio* plaque on the wall outside, the signed entrance to the accompanying *Playa Privada* car park, and the two metres of green privet-style hedge that many of them have planted to hide the front door from prying eyes. By night, look for neon. My local love hotel always makes me laugh as I walk past: in the entrance to the car park there is a massive white statue of a naked woman with her legs spread, and plenty of signs sporting shocking pink, white and black logos of riding crops — well, it is called *La Fusta* (The Riding Crop) in honour of the classy polo grounds just blocks away. Wonderful! If you fancy trying the love hotels of Buenos Aires, then the website **hotelesalojamiento.com.ar** could be a good place to start your research.

Lovers

A few tiny tips for those who decide to do more than dance:

•   Girls, the Argentine men can be cute, the tango connections can be heady, and hundreds of foreign women come and go every week. If you can handle rejection the morning after, the milonga after, the week after, after you leave – as I would say in Sallycat Spanglish, *No problemo* (in Castellano it'd be *No hay problema*, of course). But if you're the sensitive, fall-hard-and-fast type, maybe give it a bit of thought before racing towards the sunset and the nearest love hotel with the most charming man in the milonga... could it be that he's charming because he's well practised and knows that you're leaving soon? Yes, it could.

•   Girls and boys, remember that a coffee invite, whether you are making it or receiving it, doesn't necessarily mean coffee.

•   Would-be lovers who are still at the flirting stage, can indicate their intent to step things up a gear by dancing many tandas with their beau throughout the session, or can shift things into top gear by

dancing multiple consecutive tandas. Dancing multiple consecutive tandas is Tanglish for *I want you, now!*
•   In La Viruta on Friday and Saturday nights, lovers can kiss in the dark during the penultimate tango of the night (at around 6am), when the lights get switched off.
•   Lovers can grab a few hours in a love hotel when the milonga ends, if neither has a convenient apartment to head to or if either party wants to keep a private life private. If they want to keep their liaison a secret, then they might prefer to leave the milonga separately, as most Argentines do.
•   Female lovers or *novias* (girlfriends) of Argentine men might have to convince their new partner of the normality (in their foreign culture) of dancing with other men, heading out to night-time milongas with their mates, and accepting invitations to coffee from foreign male friends. However, in my own hard-won experience, all can be solved with negotiation. Lovers *can* find lasting amor in Argentina: I met my own precious soul, Carlos, in La Glorieta, and years on, we are still together. It's not always just love hotels and morning-after cold shoulders. Honest.
•   Lovers, a trip to a love hotel can be FUN. Try it!

Milongueros

What or who exactly in Buenos Aires is a milonguero? That is the question.

When I'd been here a few months, I rather publicly (on the World Wide Web) referred to myself as *la milonguera inglesa* (an English, female version of a milonguero). Of course, I'd carefully looked up the definition of the word in the marvellous Wikipedia at **en.wikipedia.org** (because it wasn't in my enormous Spanish-English dictionary) and had found the following:

Milonguero — a person whose life revolves around dancing tango and the philosophy of tango.

At that time, it was true that I thought of virtually nothing else other than tango and was indulging myself in visiting the milongas of Buenos

Aires every single night. But, I think, in my childlike enthusiasm for all things tango, I must have forgotten to read any depth at all into that particular statement or to read on to the next part of the definition[2], which said:

A title given by other tango dancers to a man (woman) who has mastered the tango dance and embodies the essence of tango.

Result? A few folk suggested to me that there might be a bit more to being a milonguero or milonguera than just turning up to a few milongas. They had a point. For sure, the men I now think of as the most authentic milongueros of Buenos Aires are the ones who've been listening to tango music and dancing tango in the milongas for longer than I've been alive. The oldest man I ever danced with in Buenos Aires was eighty-nine. The vals tanda in his arms was exquisite. I later discovered he'd been dancing for seventy-two years. He took his first tango steps in the year 1937. He was immaculate in his understated beige suit. In two hours at the matinée milonga, he only left his seat to dance twice. He was greeted on arrival by the hostess and a few of the older gentlemen, drank a tiny coffee at his table, listened to the music, watched the dancers and eventually cabeceo-ed me. I was breathless by the time he returned me to my seat. As we danced, I heard the music through my ears, but I felt every single note played through him too. How many times in seventy-two years must he have listened to those valses? How many times had he danced with his soul and the music for the woman in his arms? How many times had he escorted a woman back to her seat and left her feeling that she was the most beautiful dancer on earth? Was he a milonguero? I reckon, yes.

And yet we all have different perspectives and points of view. I once asked a social-tango-dancing Argentine friend, *What's a milonguero?* And his reply was along the lines of, *Someone who dances lots of tango in the milongas.* I forged on with, *That's a tanguero isn't it?* But he said simply, *They're the same,* and returned to his coffee and his newspaper.

---

[2]Definition supplied by anonymous Wikipedia contributors. 'Milonguero.' *Wikipedia, The Free Encyclopedia.*

I guess we each bring our own experience to the words we use, and to the weight we give to them. While I sweat over delivering up the right definition of the word *milonguero* to you, my Argentine friend just thinks of people who dance tango when he hears it.

Truthfully, in my few short years watching the many and varied men and women of the milongas of Buenos Aires, I have not yet come up with my own slick definition of either a milonguero or a milonguera. And as to whether I'll ever be one myself? Well, maybe by the next edition of **Happy Tango**, I'll know.

Music

Tango music is everything to the milongueros and milongueras of Buenos Aires. *Everything.* The maestros say that the dance of tango is what happens when the tango music passes through the ears to the soul to the feet... the dance begins with the music... what you dance depends entirely on what the music does to your soul. The locals choose their regular milongas in part because they favour the music the resident DJ plays. Their choice of partner is influenced by the orchestra playing, and they would never line anyone up without hearing the music first. If they don't see a potential dance partner who can do justice to the music, they may not dance to it at all.

There are other reasons why Argentine dancers might sit out a tango or a tanda: maybe it was a lost love's favourite; maybe it was their parents' love song; perhaps it doesn't resonate with their soul. Can foreigners ever truly understand what tango music means to an Argentine? I dance tango to beautiful music that I heard for the first time when I was in my forties, but the Argentines might be dancing to their histories, their childhood memories, the soundtracks to their lives. Local men will wait between tangos in a tanda, listen and prepare before offering me their embrace; local men will sing snippets of tango in my ear, without even realising they do it (I'm told that the women also sing to their dance partners); local men will tell me with passion about the orchestras they love, and occasionally, to my delight, they will tell me that they choose me because I feel the music too.

It wasn't always so. When I first arrived in the Buenos Aires milongas, a five-month-old UK tango baby, I wasn't a fan of traditional tango music at all: most of the 'old tango music' (as I called it) sounded the same to me, and in Britain I'd quite honestly preferred dancing to electronic tango such as Gotan Project (**gotanproject.com**) and even to non-tango pop tracks like one of my all-time favourite tunes Bedshaped by Keane (**keanemusic.com**), rather than to the scratchy original recordings of Pugliese kindly donated to me by an experienced tango-dancer friend.

Familiarity (and my observations of the relationship between the locals, their tango music and their dance) changed everything: night after night in the Buenos Aires milongas (Traditional, Tourist-circuit and even Informal) I heard the same 'old' tango, milonga and vals tracks over and over again and before I knew it I realised that some of it was dragging me out of my seat by the heart; I began to have favourite orchestras; I began to feel the music instead of just hear it; I began to love tango music in all its multilayered, intricate glory; and I began to see the music and the dance as one. Now I freely admit that what I used to call the 'old stuff' (often referred to by those in the know as the Golden Age stuff) has become *the only stuff* for me and I don't like dancing tango to non-tango music: a few electronic tango tracks can be fun, but pop music... even though it might be fabulous, it just feels empty to my tango-heart, and my soul doesn't have a desire to create the dance that I know as Argentine tango from it.

Will you hear pop tracks or alternative music played in tango venues in Buenos Aires? In the majority of places, rarely – except in the cortinas, when everyone sits down. Electronic tango? Yes, a few tandas in some of the Informal venues, or perhaps in a very occasional tanda elsewhere. But in the most Traditional milongas, absolutely none whatsoever.

Love dancing to music that you know well? Then make sure you get familiar with a few of the orchestras that you're likely to hear in Buenos Aires. Five of my personal favourites are De Angelis, Caló, D'Arienzo, D'Agostino and Biagi. Five loved by my friends are Pugliese, Tanturi, Canaro, Di Sarli and Troilo. Get a handle on a few of those ten and you feel more at home because you will hear them again and again.

How can you find out more about some of these orchestras? Try the brilliant websites **todotango.com** and **milonga.co.uk** or see Michael Lavocah's book ***Tango Stories: Musical Secrets*** (available from **tangomusicsecrets.co.uk**). And, if you want to further deepen your understanding of tango music, you could check out Joaquín Amenábar's ***Tango: Let's dance to the music!*** (**joaquinamenabar.com**).

If you want to get to grips with tango lyrics and so add another whole layer of meaning into the mix, **tangodc.com** and **planet-tango.com** offer wonderful collections of tangos in Castellano, with their English translations. Of course, tango lyrics are peppered with Lunfardo (the language created by the lower classes in Buenos Aires around the turn of the last century), and if you want to know more of that, you could visit the website **elportaldeltango.com** where there is a super Lunfardo dictionary.

In Buenos Aires, tango music to buy on CD is plentiful. You could start at Zivals music and book store, on the corner of Corrientes and Callao. Afterwards, walk down Corrientes towards the Obelisco and you'll find a large Musimundo shop, as well as many smaller places selling music. You can also talk to the DJs in the milongas. If you like the music they play, ask if they have a CD for sale, because they often do; or if you like a particular track and would like to know the title or the orchestra, they will usually be happy to enlighten you. There is also a radio station, La 2x4 at FM92.7, dedicated to tango; head to **la2x4.gov.ar** and listen online.

The 2008 film directed by Miguel Kohan, ***Café de los Maestros***, which can be tracked down by searching at **cinemanet.com.ar**, helped me to feel the music too.

Navigation

The dance floors of Buenos Aires can be like sarc

Male friends tell me the situation can be a hu;
how can you dance your usual dance when you
steps and constantly avoid banging into the (
you? Tricky.

Leaders, you're probably going to have to remember **Rule 7: Leave your expectations behind**, and forget any grand ideas of impressing the clientele of Salón Canning with boleos, ganchos, volcadas and colgadas (regardless of how much dosh you've just spent on learning them in a Tango God's seminar down the road). Sorry, but you'll be inching around the dance floor like the rest of us, and learning why many folk here dance in very close embrace. If you want to prepare before you leave home, draw a metre squared box on the floor and practise being creative! That's exactly what you might be doing in Buenos Aires, while shifting the box along in unison with the whole population of the dance floor, and protecting your partner from knocks at all times. Followers will need to get used to keeping their free leg close, and its foot on the floor: if boleos are led, keep them low and very conservative, because even if your partner has spotted a bit of space, another couple could unexpectedly move into it — I've suffered a few nasty cuts and bruises and thus learned the hard way, and I'd rather you didn't have to do the same.

Being a woman and not having learned to lead, I have no idea how hard it must be to try to navigate a crowded Buenos Aires dance floor for the first time. As the follower, if I don't feel safe and protected, I'll tense up and start watching out for the next collision (not good for soul to soul connections). If a follower keeps being knocked and kicked and shoved... well, she might just decide to say *Gracias*, and leave you stranded.

I asked one of my British friends for his thoughts on what it's like to come to Buenos Aires as a tourist and navigate the dance floors. I love his positive attitude:

> "For the tourist used to almost empty floors, the traditional milongas are the pressure cookers. It's worse if you've spent half the night getting your first cabeceo: when you finally step on to the floor, you don't want to screw up. The smart and capable dancer keeps near the outside edge, buffered front and rear by experienced dancers. Respect them, don't try to command too much space, and you will never feel more than a brush of a ̶eve. Draw inspiration from those around you, dance tight and ̶ r and keep moving. The inner lanes and middle may be ̶ (if you feel a lack of space in the outside lane)... but

don't do it! Once you relinquish your outermost position, it's gone. In the middle go the crazy undisciplined dancers and bewildered tourists. There you are vulnerable to collisions from all sides, and nobody will see you dance, apart from those who will judge you poorly for taking the easy path. The second lane (which sometimes exists on the inside of the outer lane) is fairly good, because you will have a wall of veteran dancers outside you who are not likely to cut into your path, but there is more to keep track of: the outside lane and the chaos in the middle... At the most permissive end of the venue spectrum, places such as Villa Malcolm and Práctica X scarcely seem to have any rules at all, and you must dance confidently in order to mark out your space. Try not to kick anyone, and rely on the dazzling array of talent around you to ensure the same. While these venues allow one to express the most personal freedom, they lack the predictability of the traditional places. I find that the informal environments are more stressful than the traditional milongas precisely because you must always be avoiding other dancers. In all cases, it's a good idea to try and dance with an awareness of those around you, rather than focusing entirely on yourself and your partner."

No, gracias

In Buenos Aires tango the great news is that everyone has the right to appreciate and exercise **Rule 9: Know that you can say *No***. I think that the cabeceo is kind both to those who want to say *No* and to those who are rejected. The verbal invitation on the other hand is not.

The cabeceo *No*

In this case, *No* is between the two parties involved and no-one else. We might not like the fact that we are ignored or refused, but at least the whole room doesn't have to know about it.

How do we say *No*, but leave the door open for a future *Yes*?

• A man says *No* to a woman by not looking at her in the first place. He's not actually refusing an invitation because women can't invite men, but if a woman stares at a man she's declaring her interest; if he looks away as soon as he catches her eye, she'll suspect he isn't interested. She might *want* him to invite her, she might glance away and then look back at him to make absolutely sure, but if he remains looking the other way, she can be pretty certain she isn't in his sights. For now at least, he has said *No, not interested*. In this way, he has the power.

• A woman can say *No*, and she does it similarly, by not looking at the man at all, or by looking away quickly and resolutely when she catches him looking at her. A man can stare at a woman all night, but if she doesn't return his gaze, she's not interested. In this way, she has the power.

• Not interested in dancing with a particular person? Never look at that person. Easy. Or if your eyes land on them and they are looking at you, just look away and don't look back. Everyone has power!

Why does all this apparent *No* behaviour leave the door open?

No invitation has been made. There has been no final refusal. Until the point of the invitation, a lack of interest doesn't necessarily mean *No for the whole night* or *No for life*, and both parties know it. For example, I might look the other way because I don't want to dance with a particular man for this tanda of Di Sarli, but maybe I do want to dance with him for vals, or for Pugliese, or later when I've finished the hot cup of coffee that has just been delivered to my table. Perhaps I'm sticking to my **Rule 1: Only accept or invite a person you have observed dancing**, and I want to see him dance first. Later, if the circumstances change, I can look his way again. And vice versa.

However, if both of us persist in our *No* behaviours (looking the other way), we will both be declaring our overall intention and the *No for now* becomes a *No in the long term*, and possibly a *No for forever*. But neither of us has deeply offended the other yet. Perhaps one day he will decide that my dancing has improved, or he'll have seen me around for long enough, and he might start trying to catch my eye: then I can decide if I want to hold his gaze. Maybe I'll have watched him dance by then and like what I see. Perhaps we will finally want each other at the same time and *No* will at last become *Yes!*

When does *No* mean *No* and shut the door on the possibility of *Yes*?

There is a *No* that means *NoNoNo* and will almost certainly turn into *No for forever*: the man actually invites me with a nod or a mouthed *Bailamos?* and I look away. Even if it's just between the two of us and no-one else is watching, he's put his neck on the line and invited me, and I've turned him down. He knows I mean *No, absolutely not.* There's no escaping the truth for either of us. He will probably never invite me again. I probably don't want him to.

In truth, we will both do our best never to get to this point. That's why either we play the game of look, look away, look, look away, look, invite, or we stare at each other with resolve, so that there is no doubt prior to the invitation. We want to make our intentions clear, and you can avoid confusion by doing the same.

The verbal invitation *No*

The verbal invitation is high risk. If it's made and refused, the whole room might know about it because the man has approached the woman and he then has to back away alone. *No* in this situation must surely feel like *NO!NO!NO!* to the man. Grim.

I hate saying *No* to verbal invitations because I know it can't be easy for the guy, but if the cabeceo was an alternative, I do wonder why he didn't use it — or at least its preliminaries — before deciding whether or not to invite me. If he had, he would have seen that I wasn't interested, and he would never have invited me in the first place. Then I wouldn't have had to say *No.*

Certainly, both parties can end up feeling very uncomfortable after a *No* to a verbal invitation, especially if either of them are tourists. Argentine men weigh it all up very carefully before wading in with a verbal invite. A few (the bottom feeders) will know that they're putting foreign women under pressure with this method, and their skins will be very thick. Tourists can take it far harder, especially if they come from cultures or milongas where women tend to say *Yes*. In Britain, as a woman I felt under pressure to say *Yes*. Here I don't. It feels more honest to me, and I like that. In Buenos Aires you can dance with who you *really* want, as long as they want to dance with you. Surely the Happiest Tango experiences on the dance floor are then possible. If pressure or duty is involved, then I think that the quality of the tango is compromised, or at least it is for me.

Because I'm British, I feel it's polite to turn a verbal invitation down with a smile and a *No, gracias*. In Buenos Aires, other women may not be as kind. It's possible that an unwanted verbal invitation might simply be ignored. Boys, I imagine that's a bit tough to take. My advice is to assess the situation thoroughly before wading in, and be prepared to back off with dignity if you don't get the response you want.

Non-tango tandas

Milonga and vals

Tandas of milonga (the music/dance) are played at intervals during the milonga (the social dance event). Confusing to beginners? I reckon so. Vals (the music/dance) tandas are also played at regular intervals.

Experienced tangueros and tangueras sitting in a Buenos Aires milonga will, of course, spot whether the first notes of a given tanda are tango, milonga or vals. Basically, for the complete novices among us, the milonga music sounds more like a quick 1 2 1 2 instead of the slower 1 2 3 4 (5 6 7 8) of tango music or the lilting 1 2 3 1 2 3 of vals music. Or at least, that is how I tell the difference, being of very simple musical mind.

Folks here definitely have their favourite partners for milonga and vals, yet fewer people dance the milonga tanda: there's usually a bit more space on the dance floor for that one. If it's your thing, there are some fabulous milonga dancers on the pistas of Buenos Aires. Vals is my thing! I love it and I have my favourite partners for it. I can feel quite heartbroken if a vals tanda plays and I do not get the opportunity to dance with someone who truly loves it too.

As to the frequency of these tandas throughout the session, there are usually around three or four tandas of tango, then a milonga tanda, three or four tandas of tango, then a vals tanda, so that every eight or ten tandas, you will have the opportunity to dance milonga or vals. If you want to be ready to stare with intent at favourite partners for these non-tango tandas, then keep count, get your cabeceo in as soon as the music starts, and don't miss out on a note.

Canyengue

If you see people dancing in an unusual embrace (man's left hand and woman's right hand down near the man's waist), with bent knees and both heads facing the same way, to music that might sound to the uninitiated like slow tango... you are watching canyengue as it is danced, by a small minority, in Buenos Aires today.

If you don't dance it, or indeed if you have no idea what I am talking about, you don't need to worry, as most men stepping on to the floor during the canyengue tanda will just dance tango to it. Those who do want to dance canyengue will probably choose to do so with their regular partners. Thus, women aren't generally expected to dance canyengue-style, and men can choose.

I've been fortunate enough to befriend a guy in Buenos Aires who loves to dance canyengue, and he has given me the chance to try it: at first it felt strange, but I have grown to love its grounded vibe. Just in case you'd like to know a little more, my Aussie mate and canyengue fan says in his own inimitable way:

> "Candombe and canyengue are the grandparents of what is commonly danced as tango. The fast candombe from African slaves blended some South American rhythms, plus canyengue from the sailors and gauchos. Initially the guys danced womenless

in the poor districts. Now imagine mixing all that in with some prostitutes... what a combo, people — you want fritters with that? Candombe tunes include African drumbeats, and quite a few canyengue songs feature the German tuba (think oom pa pa pa, oom pa pa pa). As the story goes, candombe slowed down to meld into milonga, and from milonga came tango. Apparently, the canyengue style of bent back and knees, stepping rather than walking or pivoting, and holding the forward hands on the man's waist, stems from the desire of the pre-1900 generation to mock the wealthy, who shunned the new dance and who danced the waltz upright on lovely wooden floors; bending to hold the woman tightly broke the waltz taboo of no emotional connection; and the poverty stricken had no polished wooden floors out in the backyards where pivoting and gliding were impossible. The heavy tread suited the poor surroundings, as well as sticking it up the wealthy."

Chacarera

In some milongas, there will be an opportunity to dance the chacarera: it's one of the famous folk dances of Argentina. If you don't know how, then it's probably best to stay in your seat and soak up the joy on the dancers' faces. I love to notice the eye contact between partners, the confidence in the women's postures, the way the most skilled men beat the sides of their feet on the floor. It's cool how women often dance together when no male partner is available, and that everyone joins in, whatever their skill level, as long as they know the basic pattern of the dance. If you do, and you have a partner, you can have a go, too. Otherwise, you could try a chacarera class (available in some of the tango schools listed in **Appendix A: 10 Tango Schools**).

A few milongas offering a chacarera tanda are La Milonga de los Consagrados, La Milonguita, Sueño Porteño, La Viruta on Friday and Saturday, and El Arranque. Additionally, if you want to see the chacarera and other Argentine folk dances being danced by locals in the street, then I strongly recommend a trip to my favourite Buenos Aires street market, Feria de Mataderos (see **See** in **Part 4** for details).

Tropical and beyond

The Argentines adore dancing to tropical tunes — well, Carlos calls them tropical (others call them Latin, and here they are known as *otros ritmos*) — merengue, cumbia, salsa... plus sometimes there's paso doble, rock or swing. Some of the milongas have a few tandas of this stuff thrown in, so don't be surprised, and if you head to milongas that are further out of town, there will likely be more of it. I like to watch the zillions of different dancing styles, the oldest folks giving it their all, and the smiles on the faces of the dancers. Get out there on the floor with the locals who know how to enjoy themselves, or just sit back and soak up this unusual aspect of selected Buenos Aires milongas.

Observation

To observe is so important that I made it **Rule 1: Only accept or invite a person you have observed dancing**.

Observing protects women and men from walking into the arms of their worst nightmare: dancing with the most undesirable dancer in the room. They might plod off the beat rather than dance on it, they might have an embrace that is going to break your back, or they might throw you or drag you around as if you are a puppet. If it's a man, he'll struggle to get dances with the locals, the regulars and the women who fell into his clutches the week before... and so, he'll make a beeline for you, the newbie. He might use the cabeceo, or he might approach your table and make a verbal invitation. In your desperation to dance or in your anxiety about saying *No*, you might say *Sí*, and it'll be too late to change your mind when you find his dancing is not up to the mark. If on the other hand, you watch the dancers for a while before saying *Sí* to anyone, all that can be avoided.

Whether you are male or female, why be in a rush? Why not sit back and take a look at the dancers in the room?

- See whether there are any dancers you would like to invite or accept: their style, their musicality, their height, their build, the expression on their face, the expression on their partner's face.
- Spot other people's favourites: one of my tanguera girlfriends always looks for the best female dancer in the room and watches who *she* chooses — they might be cool guys to give the mirada to.
- Notice the dancers you might want to avoid. Then avoid them!

In a busy venue, it can be extremely difficult to observe effectively. You might be able to pick someone out that you like the look of, but then you've got to remember their face and work out where they are sitting. This is one reason why I prefer quieter milongas, or I sit out the crush and leave my dancing until the crowd clears.

Do I always observe? No I don't. I take chances of course: when he's on the front row with the most popular dancers, when I like his vibe, when The Rules fly from my head in moments of high excitement... sometimes it pays off and all is well; sometimes, alas, I end up saying to myself, *Sallycat, why don't you ever learn to obey your own bloody rules?*

Private classes

If you want to take a private tango lesson or two when you are in Buenos Aires, how can you find the perfect *profesor* or *profesora* (male or female teacher)? Here are four methods that my friends and I have successfully used:

1. You already have your favourite professional tango dancers in mind. You've seen them dance for real or you've watched them on YouTube. Search for them online, because perhaps they have a website with their contact information and details of when they will be in Buenos Aires (many often go on tour). You can also look for them in the comprehensive lists of classes and in the adverts provided every month in the Buenos Aires tango magazines (see **The Listings** in **Part 3** for the website links).
2. Take some group classes at one of the tango schools (see **Appendix A: 10 Tango Schools**) or before the milongas and prácticas

(see the individual websites detailed in **Part 3**). Many of the teachers will give private lessons too. This works well because you can check out their teaching as well as dancing skills: the two don't always go hand in hand.

3.   Wait until you have seen some exhibitions in the milongas, or even just watched people dancing socially. Friends of mine have approached the dancers whose performances they've admired and enquired about private classes.

4.   Try out a personal recommendation. Do beware of this one though, as what may suit me, may not suit you. I think it's important not to become demoralised if someone else's 'fabulous teacher' is not quite right for you; it doesn't necessarily mean that they are a terrible teacher or that there's anything wrong with you either. If anybody's teaching is making you miserable, say goodbye and move on to find a teacher-student relationship that does work for you.

When choosing a teacher, here are some things to consider:

- Does the teacher speak English? Do you speak Spanish?
- Do you want a male teacher, a female teacher or a couple?
- Private lessons are perhaps more expensive than you might expect, and the price can depend on the name and the degree of fame. You may be able to negotiate a discount for signing up for a block of private lessons, but it might be a good idea to try one first, just to make sure you will be happy to commit to more.
- It can be tempting to take classes with several different teachers in Buenos Aires, but when I tried this in my first days here (when I'd only been dancing a few months), I found that my body got confused — this way, that way, which way? In the beginning, when I was learning the basics, I found that one good and consistent private teacher was enough. On the other hand, some prefer a portfolio of teachers: her for this, him for that, them for the other.
- Definitely put quality before quantity. It can be possible to overdose on intense private lessons. If you find yourself getting frustrated because your body isn't 'getting it' in class, give yourself a break, relax, and dance for joy in the milongas instead. You might find that

when you are least expecting it, your body does the very thing that your mind could not force it to do.

Tango tourists often ask me if they need to book private classes in advance. I think it depends on the fame of the tango teacher, and how flexible you are. If you have your heart set on training with a particular Tango God or Goddess, and will be completely devastated if they are not available for your dates — do try to get in touch with them before leaving home. On the other hand, if you're happy to go with the flow... rest assured, there will always be tango teachers ready and waiting.

You can find details of my own Buenos Aires tango teacher, at the end of the book in **Sallycat's Tango Teacher**, in case you want to try him (or him and his teaching partner) for yourself.

Regular or tourist?

At some point during your stay in Buenos Aires, you might have a little run-in with a local. Most likely it will be in your own head rather than anything overt: you might feel a bit envious of the regulars who never seem to sit out a tanda all night (a male tourist mate of mine calls it 'milonguero envy'), or you might feel a bit annoyed that the popular locals never look your way. From my own experience, let me put you in the know about this regular-versus-tourist tension.

If you go to the same milonga every week, you will become a regular. The host will come to know you. You will be seated in an increasingly better location until you reach the front row (or the row of your choosing). Over time you will build a circle of regular dance partners, and you will have worked hard for them, and they for you. Eventually it will be tricky to dance with a newcomer tourist, because if you do, you might end up having to leave out, and possibly offend, one of your regulars.

Occasionally one of your regulars will choose a newcomer over you and leave you out, dropped for some tourist who has just breezed into town for a week or two! Now this has happened to me, and I'm telling you, I didn't like it one bit. In a flash I understood why the regulars of my own sex might not have been too delighted as I broke in to their scene in a similar way. I started to see things from the other, non-tourist side. Later, I realised that my regular would return to me eventually, when the tourist had gone, but it didn't stop me getting my nose put out of joint and having a moment of tourist envy.

This is one reason why some regulars might not dance with too many strangers. It is why, if you are not a regular, you will probably end up dancing with others in the same boat — visitors from other milongas or those new in town. Not a disaster, but perhaps not what you were expecting. If you want to become a regular yourself and see things from more of a non-tourist perspective, just follow the second part of **Rule 10: Go back**.

Reservations

On a busy night at Tourist-circuit and Traditional milongas, and at some of the more Informal milongas, reservations are essential for two or more people. Not sure if it's a busy night? Reserve anyway. Even if you're alone, it doesn't do any harm to reserve, and you might end up with a better seat. Sometimes places specify a time by which you must arrive in order to claim your reservation: at the Parakultural milongas in Salón Canning, it's 11.30pm. If you want to turn up late or mid-session, then usually you can't reserve. You just have to take pot luck, but people always leave after the exhibition and tables free up.

If you are heading to a popular milonga that has traditional seating (see **Seating**) for solo dancers and you are alone, then this gives you the best chance of a good seat (whether or not you have reserved): it's relatively easy for the milonga host to slot one person in. You might even get lucky and be given the front-row seat of an absent regular or a regular who's danced their fill and gone home for the night. If you want to sit with friends of the same sex, then be warned that it will be harder for the milonga host to fit you into the gaps; you are more likely to end up on a table at the back.

The most reliable method for reservations is by phone. Find current phone numbers in the Caserón Porteño Tango Map Guide; on the website of the venue, milonga or práctica; or in the milonga listings i current edition of the tango magazines (for details of all of these valuable sources of information, see **Part 3**).

Castellano you might need:

Quiero reservar una mesa para hoy a la noche para dos personas. Mi nombre es Sally. — I want to reserve a table for tonight for two people. My name is Sally.

A qué hora tenemos que llegar? — What time do we have to arrive?

Seating

One of the things I love most about the tango salóns of Buenos Aires is that I don't have to sit in a single ring of chairs around the walls of a room, like I often did in England. In this city there are tables as well as chairs! I can arrive at the milonga alone and share a table with strangers, sit privately at a table for two with my partner or a friend, or reserve a bigger table for all my friends and turn the milonga into a social night (some milongas in large salóns, where decent food is on offer, are great for that, for example Club Sunderland on a Saturday night, and La Baldosa in Salón El Pial on a Friday).

Seating arrangements at Buenos Aires milongas vary according to the character of the place. At the most Informal end of the spectrum it can be a case of you choosing your seat on arrival according to what's available and where your friends are sitting; men, women, couples and groups will all be mixed in together. In the more Traditional milongas, seating is far more structured and suits and encourages the use of the cabeceo. An example might be rows (from one to up to five-ish) of solo-dancer men down one side of the room, solo-dancer women down another side ⌐nd couples and groups at both ends.

; better than others? Well, if you are an unknown solo
ᵥ **dancers**), it definitely helps to be given a decent seat
places. If you're hidden in the far corner behind rows
ᵧy not be spotted by anyone. If on the other hand, you
two known and fabulous dancers on the front row,

perhaps people will assume that you too are a fabulous dancer and at the very least spare you a glance.

If the venue is spacious and men can get up and walk the room to seek partners, it reduces the need for a front-row seat (for both sexes): men can seek out women they know or new faces they'd like to invite, and then cabeceo from the aisles, the bar or a seat other than their own. In smaller venues, where walking the room isn't possible and chairs are crammed together, people are stuck in the seat they are given, so a position with a good view of as many potential partners as possible becomes more important.

If you become a committed regular in a particular milonga (especially in the busy Traditional milongas, where formal rows of seating for solo dancers are the norm), it's good to always sit in the same seat. Your regular partners will get used to looking for you there. If you decide to sit somewhere other than your usual spot, and the salón is hectic, you might find that your regulars don't notice you.

How do you get a better seat over time? Follow **Rule 10: Stay late. Go back.** Make friends with the host, dance well and become a regular. Even on a short holiday of a couple of weeks, you might get a better seat the second time you visit, if the host remembers you from the week before. However, you do also have to follow **Rule 8: Be realistic.** In milongas like Cachirulo on a Saturday night and in all the El Beso milongas, it can take regulars (whether Argentines or foreigners) months to obtain a seat on the front row. I imagine there is a waiting list inscribed in the host's head: when one regular leaves town (or dies), everyone shifts up one; random tourists passing through for just one night can only expect the third row back at one of the ends of the room, unless it's a slack night in the low season.

Serious offence

The kind of scenario that might entitle you to say *Gracias* and abandon your dance partner mid-tanda is rooted in sexual and/or dangerous behaviour on the dance floor:

- Women, in the case of your male partner: we're talking groping, his mouth finding your lips or your neck, hip grinding, a super-painful embrace, repeated crashes into other couples or the furniture.
- Men, in the case of your female partner: inappropriate sexual behaviour is so unlikely that I haven't heard of it, but you may occasionally encounter a dance partner who almost breaks your back, weighs you down painfully, or constantly knees you in the groin with every turn across your body (apparently all can happen).
- Everyone, a drunken partner.

A serious offence doesn't include the fact that you don't like the way someone dances... you chose them; if you were wise, you'd have followed **Rule 1: Only accept or invite a person you have observed dancing**; therefore, you dance to the end of the tanda with them. It's considered rude to abandon a partner mid-tanda. It's deeply embarrassing to be left stranded on the dance floor, because everyone will be watching. In Buenos Aires, only a serious offence justifies the action.

Shoe change

According to the códigos, women's shoes (and indeed clothes) should not be changed at the table, but in the baños. In my case, I vary my behaviour according to the venue/milonga/práctica; I'd be fibbing if I said that I always go to the restroom to change my shoes. However, I do make sure I have wet-wipes in my bag in case my hands need a clean afterwards, because I wouldn't want to touch the soles of my shoes and then the hands of a milonguero. It wouldn't be nice behaviour, would it?

In the Traditional milongas and in the more Traditional of the Tourist-circuit places, I go to the restroom. I cannot imagine sitting in the front row among elegant women, with rows of men opposite me, and changing my shoes in front of them all. In the process of bending down or raising my feet to effect the change, I could end up revealing far more than my naked ankles to the male audience on the other side of the room: knickers, bra, flesh... It could get ugly. It might also cause offence. So girls, I recommend that you pop to the baños, save your blushes, and earn the respect of the locals at the same time. Another excellent reason to change your shoes and clothes in the restroom is that you are then able to use the mirror to check you are looking your tip-top best and so make a far more glamorous entrance to the milonga — take advantage of this chance to be seen.

If I'm in a hectic Tourist-circuit venue and I'm sitting around a table with a group of friends and facing them, I might not make the trip to the restroom; frankly it gets so packed in those places that no-one can see what anyone else is doing anyway. Plus, I am now so well practised that I can swiftly carry out the shoe change under the tablecloth without even bending down, and I doubt anyone notices me. On the other hand, if I'm out alone and I want to convey my most elegant image to the solo male dancers, I pop to the restroom. For me, it's a question of judgement and I err on the side of caution, as I prefer not to offend anyone. In any case, if you do decide to change your shoes at the table, it's cool to keep it out of sight, discreet and quick.

In the Informal milongas and prácticas, the restroom trip is almost certainly not required, as things are far more relaxed. If in doubt, observe the regulars, and follow suit. Outside at La Glorieta, you'll be using one of the park benches!

Many locals, and especially the men, don't change their shoes at all in the milongas, because they arrive wearing their dancing shoes.

Shoe shopping

Once all I cared about was looks; now I dream of comfort too. And, as I've mentioned in the **Dress for success** entry, I've gone from wanting to have the glitziest shoes on the floor, to thinking more about what my shoes might be saying about me. Nowhere else provides such an incredible range of tango shoes, from practical to glittering designer gems; in Buenos Aires, you can find shoes that feel great *and* say something fantastic about you. My suggestions as to where you should start? I offer you **10 Tango Shoe Stores** in **Appendix B**, but there are plenty more, and new labels join the party every year.

Here are my top tips for buying tango shoes in Buenos Aires:

1. Get to know the brands, as some will suit the shape of your feet better than others.
2. Visit a few shops before parting with any cash. The design choice is spectacular: you might see a fabulous shoe in one store on Monday, but an even more fabulous one in another place on Tuesday.
3. Check out the quality of materials and craftsmanship: some shoes have cardboard inners, which can crack under pressure, and some have leather inners, which don't; do satisfy yourself that the shoes you are about to buy have been well made.
4. Consider what the sole is made of: rubber (good for slippery floors), leather (good for sticky floors) or tough suede (which seems to work well in between). There are clever solutions, like the 2x4alpie shoes for men that offer all three soles in an interchangeable system.
5. Appreciate the risks of having a shoe made for you, and establish in advance whether you are committed to buying the shoe if it turns out to be less than you'd wished for. For both men and women, it may sound great that you can pick this leather and that heel, but can you really know until you see it all together and try it on, that it isn't going to look like a dog's dinner and squeeze your bunion?
6. Sometimes there is a discount for *efectivo* (cash) or for bulk purchases. Or there may be a charge for using a *tarjeta de crédito* (credit card). Sometimes you can only pay with cash, so don't assume that you can use a card.
7. Use the Caserón Porteño Tango Map Guide to plan your shoe shopping expeditions. Several shoe stores are marked on the map already. You can add others yourself, and thus plan an efficient route around the emerging clusters of shops. Time saved travelling is precious time for trying on more shoes and/or dancing.

And a few extra tips for the ladies:

1. It's definitely better to buy on the tight (but still comfortable) side because many of the gorgeous fabrics stretch with wear. If you're only going to use them now and again, it's less of a concern.
2. In Comme il Faut, there aren't many shoes on display and the shop assistants only bring out what you ask for. This may mean that

you will miss out on the most beautiful shoe they have because you asked for a particular colour. Suggest a range of options; shop with friends so that you see more shoes; and be happy to share the sofas with other customers because you can glimpse what they're trying on!

3.   Think about wear and tear. I have found patent leather to be fabulous, and fine fabrics to be awful. On early shoe shopping trips I got all excited about the wacky pale and lacy options available in Buenos Aires and forgot that dirt can't be wiped off lemon-yellow silk.

4.   Before you leave the shop, make sure that there are sufficient holes in the ankle straps. It's gutting to go to wear your shoes for the first time and discover that you have to start stabbing them with a sharp screwdriver.

Sitting out

When I arrived here, I wanted to dance. Correction: I was *desperate* to dance, every tanda of every night! In Britain, I'd developed the notion that if I was left sitting out for even a tanda, I was undesirable, a terrible dancer, destined to fester on the British tango scrapheap forever.

In the more Traditional milongas of Buenos Aires, as long as you follow **Rule 4: Exude magnetic energy** at all times, and look relaxed, no-one will think that you are on the tango scrapheap if you sit out a few tandas, whether you are male or female. Rather, they will assume that you are not dancing for your own reasons. Of course, if you sit for hours and don't dance, it's a different matter (particularly, I am sorry to say, if you are a woman), but my point is that in Buenos Aires it isn't at all unusual for people to sit tandas out. Some (especially older men in the more Traditional places) go to the milonga, sit and listen to the music, eat, drink, talk and dance just a few tandas in total. In the more Informal places, groups of friends might not dance that much either. It seems quite common for people to sit and chat, have a drink, watch the dancers and relax. It's true that in the Informal venues you might stand out more if you sit on your own and don't dance much... being part of a group tends to help with **Rule 5: Look the part** in these places.

Men new in town sometimes feel sorry for a woman who appears not to be dancing: they invite her and she refuses — and they wonder why. But there are so many reasons why someone might be not dancing (read the **No, gracias** entry to see what I mean). If I don't want to dance, I try to indicate it by not looking around at the men, keeping my eyes on the dancing couples, drinking my coffee, focusing on my friends. A man or a woman behaving like this is clearly indicating that they are not going to dance, are not planning on giving or accepting a cabeceo, and are not going to be sympathetic to a verbal invitation either; you will probably get rejected if you try one.

If you are only in Buenos Aires for two weeks, then of course I understand that you might want to dance as much as possible, but it's as well to know in advance that the locals and regulars don't exhibit the same sense of urgency.

Smoking

It's been a case of No Smoking inside the city's tango salóns since 2006, when smoking was banned in public places in Buenos Aires, though a few venues allow it on their balconies and in the entrance halls (in winter). If there is no balcony and no sign of smokers anywhere indoors, then it's outside on the street, whatever the weather.

Solo dancers

A solo dancer is a tanguero or tanguera who chooses to go out to dance on their lonesome: they will sit *solo* (men) or *sola* (women) at the milonga; in the Traditional venues most women will sit in the women's section, and most men in the men's section. By choosing to sit as a solo dancer, you are clearly declaring your intention to invite and accept other solo dancers. You are also showing that you mean business: you haven't turned up with a group of friends to chat and socialise; you're there to listen to the music and dance; other solo dancers, who might not have looked your way if you'd arrived in a group, will look at you now.

Couples who want to dance with others in the most Traditional milongas of Buenos Aires will have to split up and sit solo (see **Couples** for more details).

If you walk into a milonga on your own, the host will always ask you if you are alone, so that he or she knows where to seat you. Check out the **Hosts and organisers** entry for details of the conversation you will have.

Sorteo

In some Traditional milongas there will be a *sorteo* (raffle) for prizes such as champagne, a CD, a pair of tango shoes, a pizza... Your raffle ticket is your entry ticket, which will be numbered, or your entry ticket will be exchanged for a numbered ticket on the way in. The draw will take place fairly late on in the session. If you win, don't leap up and run to the host. Wave and call out *Sí!* Then wait for the host to come to you for the ticket and eventually, with your prize.

Good luck or *Suerte* (as they say in Argentina!).

Styles of tango

If I ask Carlos, my Argentine partner, what style of tango he dances, he will say, *My own.* If I push him for more details he might name his hero Carlos Gavito and he might mention Carlos Pérez whose group classes he once attended. If you asked me what style of tango I dance, I'd say, *My own, but exactly how I dance will depend on my partner's style and the space available to both of us — I adapt my style to suit my partner's unique dance.* I think that there are as many styles of tango in Buenos Aires as there are people dancing here in any given moment.

Labels do exist for tango styles though, don't they? You might have heard of some of them. Tango milonguero, tango salón and tango nuevo are probably the labels most commonly spoken of in Buenos Aires; if you decide to research tango schools or tango teachers here, you will certainly see them being used in an attempt to define the style of tango being taught, but you will need to bear in mind that they might mean different things to different people from different countries, or even to different tango teachers in the same country, including teachers in Argentina. If you come here with a desire to learn a particular tango style, I suggest either that you seek out a tango school which states that it teaches that style (and confirm with them exactly what *they* mean by the style label they use), or that you track down a teacher who dances in the style you like. If you don't have a particular style in mind, you can take heart from my own story, as it proves that you can still end up a pretty competent Argentine tango dancer even if you haven't got a clue what the various labels mean.

When I took up tango, I just thought of it as tango. I went to a beginners' class of Argentine tango in the south of England and began to learn to walk backwards. When I came to Argentina I found my tango teacher Ariel by pure chance (via the travel experience I signed up for on the internet with Travellers Worldwide at **travellersworldwide.com**) and I started to learn to walk backwards all over again. To me it was still just tango. After I'd been here about six months, a North American tango tourist asked me what style of tango I was learning: I remember feeling mortified, as if I should have known, as if I should have had a slick and straightforward answer for him. Later I talked to Ariel and began to appreciate where his unique tango style had come from: his many teachers, dancers he'd admired and observed, and his personality. He was reluctant to put a label on his own style and he told me that mine would come from many places, that it would adapt to my leaders and that it would emerge and change over time. Sometimes we danced close embrace. Sometimes we danced with an open embrace. Sometimes we moved between the two. What we danced depended on the music, his mood, my mood, and the size of studio we were in. I am guessing that if we'd danced in a packed milonga, his style would have adapted and become tighter, to fit the space.

To see Buenos Aires dancing the close-embrace tango often labelled as tango milonguero, head to any of the Traditional milongas in this book and watch the majority of the locals dance. To catch a glimpse of the open-embrace tango often labelled as tango nuevo, head to Práctica X on a Tuesday night. And to get a good idea of what the Buenos Aires World Tango Championship judges think of as perfect tango salón, watch a performance on YouTube or live in Buenos Aires by any of the past champions in the Tango Salón category: in 2012, Facundo de la Cruz y Paola Sanz.

If you're interested in finding out where today's tango style-labels might have come from, take a look at Christine Denniston's thought-provoking book; it's available from **totaltango.com** and is entitled *The Meaning of Tango: The Story of the Argentinian Dance*.

Tanda

This is the set you will dance with one partner. Most often it's composed of tango music, but there'll usually be regular tandas of milonga and vals too, plus perhaps a few other non-tango tandas (see **Non-tango tandas** for details of them all).

Tango tandas are most often four tangos from the same orchestra and from the same historical period. Thus when you hear the first tango in a tanda, you will have a clear idea of the style of the whole set. This enables dancers to select a partner to match the music or to choose to sit out the tanda if they don't wish to dance it.

Between tangos in a tanda, the partners stop dancing, move out of the embrace, and stand and chat, or smile politely at each other for around fifteen seconds (see below for the explanation) as the next piece of music plays. This break grants the dancers a chance to adjust to the new music before entering the embrace to dance again. It isn't the done thing to touch your partner during this break, unless you are lovers and you want everyone to know it. Do be aware that Argentines might stand quite close to you: sometimes I find myself stepping backwards to maintain my personal space, and I also back away at hands resting on my arm or any other part of me during the break. It doesn't seem to cause offence.

Between tangos, topics of conversation tend to be: the music, the venue, how busy the milonga is — *Hay mucha gente* (There are lots of people), how hot or cold it is — *Hace calor/frio* (It's hot/cold), and of course the most popular question to tourists is, *De dónde sos?* (Where are you from?). Have your answer ready. First names may be exchanged, but the etiquette is to avoid giving surnames, and not part with too many personal details either... it protects privacy. Men might give a few *piropos* (over-the-top, but often wonderfully poetic compliments, which can be called out in the street by strangers, as well as whispered on the dance floor); these should be taken with a pinch of salt and a smile: *You dance like a porteña*, especially! Lovely piropos I've had have included: *I can die now I've danced with you; you are the only woman in the room who knows how to walk; you are so light I feel you as a feather; this is the orchestra that makes me tremble and I have saved it for you.*

Be aware that talking about the other milongas you attend (or asking your dance partners about the milongas they attend) could be viewed as a come-on: be a bit vague, unless you want to appear keen. In discussions about the effects of the weather, make sure you stick to *Tengo calor* (I'm hot, as in temperature), and avoid saying *Estoy caliente*, which means I'm hot, as in sexually. If you don't want to talk or you don't speak Castellano, you can just smile at your partner. It works just fine.

Men who are in the know will prepare to dance the next tango in the tanda around fifteen seconds after the music starts playing. This is because (I am informed by a male-dancer friend and tango music aficionado) Golden Age tangos have an introduction of around fifteen seconds. The locals naturally sense the end of the intro and move back into the embrace, ready to dance again as the 'tango proper' starts. So, newbies who want to join the knowledgeable throng (apparently only the least experienced and poorest dancers set off too soon) should count while they chat. If talking Spanish to a stranger and counting to fifteen elephants at the same time is too much multi-tasking, just wait until the majority of those around you resume the embrace, then follow suit. Personally, I think it can often be even longer than fifteen seconds before the mass is moving again, so you can take your time without risk.

It's polite to dance the entire tanda, from the point that you started it, with your partner, and it's rude to say *Gracias* and abandon your partner before the tanda ends, unless a serious offence occurs (see

Serious offence). Sometimes men will invite, and women will accept, unknown partners midway through the tanda to minimise the risk of having to endure four tangos with someone who can't dance. If someone says *Gracias* to you mid-tanda and leaves you stranded, I'm afraid it means that you've offended them. It has happened to me once only, to my horror, after only a few seconds of a tanda of milonga, and the *Gracias* was accompanied by the words, *I thought you said you danced milonga!* I was mortified and sat down with a red face, but I'd only myself to blame: he'd invited me verbally at the table, and I'd accepted without seeing him dance or sussing him out. Mind you, his behaviour was pretty uncool. He'd picked me without observing me; I am not that terrible at milonga; and he might have given me more than five seconds. Needless to say, I won't be giving *him* the mirada in the future. And neither will any of my friends.

So, in your eagerness to be polite and friendly after a tango straight from heaven, avoid thanking your partner after the first dance in the tanda – you might find they start walking back to their seat, with a very confused and hurt expression on their face and a mark against you in their heart; instead, bite your tongue and wait until you hear the cortina music before uttering the word *Gracias*. The cortina signals the end of the tanda, and *that's* the moment to thank your partner. Say *Gracias*, or if you enjoyed it, *Muchas gracias*. If you really enjoyed it, *Muy lindo* (Really lovely) or *Un placer* (A pleasure) will be well received. Ladies, it's quite normal for the men to escort you back to your table with a hand on your shoulder, or some such caring gesture.

How many tandas with a new partner if you are not interested in anything other than dancing? Perhaps you can get away with three, but personally I'd stick to two spread throughout the session. If I already know someone, I might dance three tandas with them over a period of a few hours, but usually one of them will not be tango, but rather vals or milonga, and I reserve this for guys I feel completely comfortable with, and who I know are not going to hit on me. On most occasions when I've danced three tandas (in my enthusiasm and delight at the way the guy dances), I've always seemed to land myself with someone who wants more than three tandas next time around. Dancing consecutive tandas with the same person is a complete no-no, unless your dance partner is already your lover, or you would like them to be, very soon. If you want to elicit a coffee invite, invites to other milongas and expectations about sex... then feel free to dance as many consecutive tandas as you like. But, the entire milonga population will probably notice.

In a few venues, tandas are not of four: in La Viruta on Fridays and Saturdays they are of six and therefore rather long, so choose your partners carefully. In some Informal places there are no cortina breaks in the music, so you have to decide when to say *Gracias* and move on to a new partner. In this situation, most people dancing with strangers would probably dance three or four numbers before saying *Gracias*. It would be a bit rude to desert a partner after one or two, but it wouldn't be a crime to dance five: Informal prácticas, especially, offer the greatest degree of flexibility. But wherever you are, do be careful not to send signals that you are interested in something other than dancing, if you are not.

Tango schools

Tango schools are places where you can choose from a schedule of group classes, try out a range of teachers if you are considering private lessons, and meet like-minded tango students who may head to the same milongas as you. Some schools state that they specialise in a particular tango style, such as milonguero, salón or nuevo (see **Styles of tango**). Ask the school to explain to you exactly what they mean by the style before you start, if it matters to you. Some schools also offer classes in milonga, vals, canyengue, folk dance, body conditioning, and yoga, among other things. Some also hold prácticas for their students. These can be great for practising what you have learned, for making friends and for finding dance partners.

Tango schools in Buenos Aires vary widely in character. Some have dedicated buildings or parts of a building, with classes running most days of the week: these may have a receptionist who can talk you through the classes on offer and give you a copy of the latest programme. Other schools may rent a space on just a few occasions during the week, and you'll have to find out those times in advance, and arrive just before the class if you want to talk to the teachers about their teaching method or the classes they recommend for your needs. Some schools will assess your level: this is usually done by a teacher dancing with you. Levels are usually labelled as *principiante* (beginner), *intermedio* (intermediate) and *avanzado* (advanced), though a few places might have numbered levels. If you need English, do not assume that it will be spoken — check first. Some schools offer discounts if you sign up for a block of classes, but there can be an expiry date, so ask about the conditions.

I haven't taken classes in a tango school for a while. Many of my friends have, and they have found the experience an excellent one. You can find ten of their current suggestions in **Appendix B: 10 Tango Schools**, though of course, there are many others too. I think it's important to follow **Rule 3: Seek out your 'tango homes'**, where tango schools are concerned. I've had my fingers burnt when I've recommended a school to a tourist, only to discover that what suits me may not suit everyone. The schools in my list offer a cross section of what is available, with respect to the style of tango being taught and the character of the place. If you fancy trying a tango school, look at the websites before you leave home, and then pay a visit to, and perhaps take a sample class in, any that you feel could be right for you. This way, you can find out whether you like the teaching and the vibe, and decide whether to opt to buy a package deal of classes. If it turns out that these places aren't your style, I am sure that once you've tried a class or two and met a few fellow students, you'll hear about somewhere else that turns out to be just perfect.

Taxi dancers

Only in Buenos Aires for a short time and want to be certain to dance the night away? Want to soak up the Traditional scene, but can't get to grips with the cabeceo? Quaking in your tango shoes at the thought of turning up at a milonga alone and then not dancing at all?

Maybe you should consider hiring a taxi dancer: a tango dancer you pay by the hour (usually for three hours) to dance with you, and only you... A good one can provide blissful tangos, be a pleasure to sit with, give you the lowdown on a few tips and tricks, show you off on the dance floor so that you can be seen by other dancers (for later, when the taxi dancer's time is up, and he or she heads off and leaves you to it), and help build your Buenos Aires tango confidence before you go it alone. You could also hire one between two or three friends, to keep the cost down, and ease the potential intensity of a one-to-one scenario with a stranger (if that bothers you).

Worried about shady goings-on? Hire your taxi dancer through an agency that does everything possible to ensure both happy clients and happy taxi dancers (try TangoTaxiDancers at **tangotaxidancers.com**), or follow a recommendation from a satisfied customer (not me, however, as I haven't ever sampled the services of a taxi dancer myself).

Unwanted attention

Perhaps it's a request for a phone number between tangos or at the end of a tanda. Perhaps it's an invite to another milonga. Perhaps it's a coffee invite. All these things are most likely a declaration of sexual interest. I guess that occasionally they may not be, but you probably have to assume they might be. If you want to demonstrate that kind of interest yourself, then play along. Often though, this sort of attention can be unwanted and annoying.

My number one strategy when I didn't have the language to say more, and when I was concerned about offending people, was to plead ignorance. I smiled sweetly and said *No comprendo* (I don't understand). I also managed *No tengo* (I don't have) when either a phone number or email address was being requested. Later, I started talking about *mi novio* (my boyfriend). Sometimes it worked, other times it didn't. Some women wear a wedding ring, even if they're not married, and point to it saying *Estoy casada* (I'm married) — but beware of mistakenly saying *Estoy cansada* (I'm tired), although by then you might be.

These guys are well practised: they might strike lucky with an occasional Yes response, but they also get a lot of Nos, so don't worry about causing offence. *No, gracias* works in most cases: if you're concerned about upsetting anyone, just smile as you say it, but you have to be prepared to be pretty firm. Some men will try it on.

No, gracias will also be needed if you start getting repeated invitations to dance from someone that you danced with in the beginning but don't want to dance with any more. You can soften it with *No por ahora, gracias* (Not just now thank you). Once you've said it a few times, they will get the message. They've probably heard it countless times before.

If you've read the entry **Serious offence**, you will know that sometimes unwanted attention can come in the form of touching of a sexual nature and that it can happen on the dance floor. I once had hip grinding in Salón Canning, and the lips of a stranger trying to find mine in La Viruta. Other possibilities are hands reaching round to a breast, or down to buttocks. Sometimes it's hard to be sure if it's really happened: perhaps in slight shock you find yourself thinking, *Did I just imagine that?* That's why I'm telling you that it does happen (occasionally), so don't assume you imagined it. How to deal with it? My choice was never to dance with those men again, and to warn my friends. A friend of mine steps back and says firmly, *Bailamos, nada más* (We're dancing, nothing more). She reports great success. Of course if the behaviour was repeated or very serious, she would walk away with a simple *Gracias* (no explanation required), and that's always an option, at any point, if you feel at all invaded or threatened.

I think there are ways to discourage this type of behaviour. Follow **Rule 1: Only accept a person you have observed dancing** and **Rule 2: Women — don't accept a verbal invitation unless you know the person or he is Pablo Veron**. Once on the dance floor, be aware and notice when you feel any kind of vibe that makes you feel uncomfortable, then present a slightly cooler-than-normal you; I've learned to conjure up my *fria* (cold) face when required, and you might need to do the same. Female tourists can sometimes be just too friendly, smiley, keen, desperate... and alas it can attract the guys who will take advantage. Being prepared is half the battle won.

Valuables

What should you take to the milonga? In an ideal world: yourself, your shoes and enough money to cover transport, entry and drinks. Then you won't need to leave things in the coat check, keep your eye on your bag, or worry about anything other than dancing. Doesn't work like that though, does it? I've usually got a bag full of paraphernalia, though the contents aren't valuable, so I never have to worry too much.

I prefer a big, obvious (usually bright and flowery) bag because I can see it easily, it won't get mistaken for anyone else's and a male thief would look pretty stupid nicking it. I never leave valuables lying on the table, whether I'm dancing or not, and I keep my bag well under the table-cloth, where a thief would have to scrabble around for it. I don't like dancing with belt-type bags tied round my body, though I've done it on occasion: they ruin an outfit, restrict my movement and mark me out as someone with valuables worth stealing. These days I prefer to follow **Rule 5: Look the part** and keep my valuables out of sight like the locals do. I'm never paranoid about my stuff getting nicked and it never has been, but I'm sensible about what I take out with me.

Verbal Invitation

The verbal invitation is definitely one of the potential banana skins of Buenos Aires tango. It's the why of **Rule 2: Women — don't accept a verbal invitation unless you know the person or he is Pablo Veron. Men — use the cabeceo.** So, how should you respond when someone asks *Querés bailar?* or *Bailás?* (Do you want to dance?).

The verbal invitation to dance is sometimes made with good intentions in Buenos Aires, and in some more Informal places it's the norm. It's also made by guys who feel uncomfortable with the cabeceo, or by those who are not in the know about the códigos or the fact that the cabeceo even exists. But men need to know that, even when made with good intentions, the answer may be *No, gracias.* Women need to remember **Rule 9: Know that you can say *No*,** and never allow themselves to feel pressured into saying *Sí*.

The verbal invitation can also be made with less than good intentions, especially in the Tourist-circuit places. Some Argentine men make verbal invitations with the express purpose of putting pressure on the woman. These bottom feeders know that in our early desperation to dance with an Argentine and because we are initially more comfortable with verbal invitations than the cabeceo, we tourist women will almost shout *Sí!* By the time we realise that we are dancing with a bottom feeder, the damage has been done: we will have to find a way to turn them down the next time and that can feel extremely awkward. Sometimes we just keep dancing with them, even though we hate the experience. Not good. And believe it or not, men may need to be on their guard too: an attractive male friend of mine reports that he was once hounded by an older Argentine woman who invited him to dance verbally several times; it's the only incidence I've heard of, but obviously it can happen.

You have to use your judgement with the verbal invitation, and this is where Pablo Veron of **Rule 2** comes in. Pablo is my Sallycat code for someone we feel we must dance with even though they ask us verbally. The Pablos do exist: the fabulous dancer you've had your eye on all night, who crosses the room to invite you; the guy who politely explains, *I've been trying to catch your eye for hours, but you've been talking to your friend, and I just cannot leave the milonga without one tanda*; the bloke who is just absolutely drop-dead gorgeous. Oh the Pablos...

Sometimes the Pablos are sent direct from heaven to deliver our Happiest Tango of the night. But then again, if your Pablo turns out to be a bottom feeder, well, don't say I didn't warn you!

Zapatos

I think I forgot to mention that the Castellano for tango shoes is *zapatos de tango*. The Castellano for shoes is *zapatos*, you see. *Zapatillas* (trainers, training shoes or sneakers), in the context of tango, are the flat trainer-style dance shoes (often called practice shoes) used by many for practising in class and, in the more Informal venues, for dancing too. Thus, it is true that not many tango travellers leave Buenos Aires without splashing their cash on something beginning with the letter Z.

Part 3

WHERE WILL YOU DANCE IN BUENOS AIRES?

The tango venues of this city host more than one hundred milongas a week, and they're just the ones the average tourist gets to hear of. A venue may hold just a single weekly milonga, or it may be home to a different one every night, each run by a different organiser and having its own unique character. The choice is vast, exciting and baffling. When I arrived in Buenos Aires, I was lucky because I had forever to discover places I liked. You might only have two weeks. Thus it's my job to make some suggestions. To begin with, I encourage you to follow **Rule 3: Seek out your 'tango homes'**.

The term 'tango home' describes a venue or a milonga where you feel relaxed, comfortable and confident. In other words, it's a place where you feel at home. All kinds of factors contribute. In general I prefer the more Traditional, but I particularly seek a friendly, welcoming vibe. Music that moves me, dancers I enjoy, a historic venue, decent coffee, good food, reasonable entry rates... all can play a part for me. Your criteria might be very different. Regardless of your preferences, I guarantee there'll be some places that you'll walk into and never want to leave, and others that'll make you wonder what all the fuss is about.

The question is: can you know if you will like a place if you don't go and see it for yourself? At a fine-tuning level, no I don't think you can, but at a broad-brush level, maybe: if you know you prefer Traditional tango and an elegant, classy salón, you should probably give Informal La Viruta on a Sunday night, with its electronic tango music, a miss. Of course, if you have months and months, then I'd have to say try everything once; but if you're short of time, don't waste valuable nights finding out what you don't like.

So, how can I help you to know which places might be your 'tango homes'?

First I'll describe **The 3 Main Categories of Venue/Milonga** that I have observed in Buenos Aires: Tourist-circuit, Traditional and Informal, with some general tips about how to conduct yourself in each of them. Then, I'll give you the lowdown on **20 Places to Try First** across the three categories, to get you started on the right track. In **Beyond the 20 with the Milonga Listings**, I'll tell you about the useful websites and magazines that detail almost all the one-hundred-plus milongas in Buenos Aires and give you information on **Finding the Tango Venues**, because I know that one day you'll want to explore further and take Buenos Aires tango to the limit. Finally, in **The Week at a Glance**, I'll chart a good selection of the milongas and prácticas that I mention, on a handy agenda, so that you can plan your first week's tango in Buenos Aires with ease.

In Buenos Aires, people may refer to milongas in several ways: the name of the milonga itself, as chosen by its organiser; the name of the venue where the milonga is held; or the address of the venue.

For example, I might say I'm going to *El Maipú*, someone else might say they are going to *La Nacional, Monday evening*, and yet another person might say they are going to *the Monday milonga at Alsina 1465* or (if the conversation is taking place on a Monday) simply to *La Nacional*. We will all end up in the same Monday evening milonga called El Maipú, in the venue known as La Nacional, at the address Alsina 1465.

I'll give you the full names of venues and milongas, but I'll also tell you the names by which places are commonly known.

The 3 Main Categories of Venue/Milonga

Over time I've noticed something about all the milongas I've been to in Buenos Aires:

1.   I can broadly categorise them into three main groups: Tourist-circuit, Traditional and Informal. Sometimes all the milongas held in a venue fall into the same category, but not always.
2.   I tend to feel most comfortable with one of the three categories, yet occasionally I enjoy a dip into the others.
3.   If I go to the places where I feel most comfortable, I am usually invited to dance and I have Happy Tango experiences: I am in one of my 'tango homes'.

Where will your 'tango homes' be? Will they be in my preferred category, will they be in a different category, or will you prefer to dance in all three?

Tourist-circuit Venues/Milongas

This is the group of venues/milongas that most tourists visit on their first trip to Buenos Aires. They're a combination of the venues and the milongas that are most famous outside of Argentina and those that are centrally located. Some have a night of the week that is known to be 'their' night: for example, even though the venue Centro Región Leonesa hosts milongas on more than one day of the week, the Thursday night milonga called Niño Bien is the most well known in this venue and is in my Tourist-circuit category. Two other famous Tourist-circuit venues are Salón Canning and Confitería Ideal. Details of these and more Tourist-circuit venues and the milongas held in them can be found in **6 Tourist-circuit Places to Try First**, later in **Part 3**.

What can you expect from the milongas in my Tourist-circuit category?

1. Lots of glammed-up tourists, but also the locals who enjoy dancing with foreigners. There's usually a mixed age range, with younger dancers tending to arrive in the early hours of the morning from the Informal venues.
2. Performances by live orchestras and professional dancers.
3. The highest entry prices, especially on live orchestra nights.
4. Mixed seating arrangements: solo dancers, couples and groups all in together; you're less likely to see the more formal rows of single-sex seating common in the most Traditional places.
5. Crowds. An advance reservation is a very good idea, and on your arrival you should wait to be seated by the host. You're likely to find packed dance floors until the orchestra has performed or the exhibition is over: many people leave after that, and it's worth staying on after they do.
6. The well-known and even the famous on show: tango professionals and tango teachers. Also, those selling anything tango related.
7. A few lecherous men (bottom feeders) who prey on tourist women, but you can manage the situation if you've read **Part 2**.
8. A mixture of the cabeceo and the verbal invitation to dance, though the cabeceo is definitely preferred by the majority of Argentines and long-stay foreigners. Men tend to walk around (cruise) the room to increase their options for the cabeceo; they move into the eye line of women who they wish to invite. Some of these milongas can therefore be good for couples who want to sit together but dance with other people too (see **Couples** in **Part 2**).
9. A wide range of dancing skills and dance styles, depending on the venue and the space available on the dance floor. Some places are more Traditional in character than others.
10. Poor floorcraft at peak times in some of the busiest milongas: lots of tourists who lack experience navigating busy Buenos Aires dance floors; lots of tourists who don't understand that on those busy

floors it's necessary to dance small, with feet in contact with the ground; lots of big and fancy moves with little concern shown for other dancers.

Here are five tips for how to get the best out of the Tourist-circuit places:

1.   Visit on nights when there is an orchestra playing or a favourite couple dancing an exhibition, and so get the fullest experience and the best value for money.

2.   If you want to dance comfortably, sit out the mid-session crush (as many locals do), and stay on after the performance, or for the final hour of the milonga: folks who only came to see the show will go, leaving the hardcore dancers behind. Seats will become available then too, so if you don't want to see the show, you could arrive late yourself.

3.   In places with mixed seating, it can be more fun to go with friends. Tables are set up so that you sit *with* people (facing them across the table), rather than in rows as in the more Traditional milongas. If you turn up alone, you might find yourself sitting at a table for four with strangers: I have met some nice people this way, so if you are the sociable type it can work out very well.

4.   **Sallycat's Rules for Happy Tango in Buenos Aires** should be carried in your head at all times. They can really save you from the most common predicaments in the Tourist-circuit places.

5.   Be aware that during the most famous tango festivals, such as CITA (Congreso Internacional de Tango Argentino, usually held in March; see **tangopal.com**) and the Buenos Aires Tango Festival y Mundial de Baile (usually in August; see **tangobuenosaires.gob.ar**), the Tourist-circuit venues/milongas are packed. Perhaps you want your visit here to coincide with a big festival, but if not, there is more space on the dance floors at other times. In the quietest months (usually June, September and January), there is far more space and a greater proportion of Argentines, but fewer dancers from all over the world and an emptier vibe.

Traditional Venues/Milongas

The first time you find yourself seated alone in one of the most Traditional milongas in Buenos Aires on a busy night, you may want to do one of two things: stare with your jaw on the floor, or run straight out the door and across the city to La Viruta.

Have you ever sat hemmed in by rows of dancers of your own sex, facing rows of dancers of the opposite sex, needing to cabeceo a partner within the first seconds of a tanda or risk your view of potential partners getting blocked by a packed dance floor? Have you ever watched banks of glamorous milongueras tossing their hair, fanning themselves at the speed of a humming bird's wings, competing for the eyes of their favourite milongueros? Have you ever clocked rows of suited, café sipping, champagne swilling, salami and cheese guzzling milongueros, leaning back in the seats that are their second homes, listening for their favourite music and then nonchalantly taking their pick of the most favoured milongueras?

No? Ah well, you must. If you come here and don't try at least one of the most high-powered, Traditional milongas in town, then I don't really think you can leave saying that you have seen it all. It could feel a little intimidating at first, so you might choose to visit with a friend and/or sit with the couples and groups. On the other hand, if you mean business as a solo dancer, then muster your magnetic energy, line up with some of the most popular milongueros and milongueras of Buenos Aires, and be prepared to compete hard for dances.

A few milongas that offer up this more serious end of the Traditional Buenos Aires tango spectrum are Cachirulo in El Beso (Tuesday) and in Club Villa Malcolm (Saturday), Lujos in El Beso (Thursday) and in Plaza Bohemia (Sunday), and El Maipú in La Nacional (Monday).

If you like the sound of this Traditional scene, but would prefer to ease yourself into it gently, then an excellent option is to try the afternoon or early-evening milongas (known as the matinée milongas). They're more accessible than their late-night counterparts, in that it's easier for newcomers to achieve successful cabeceos: you can build your confidence before joining the late-night crowd. Many newcomers start in Nuevo Salón La Argentina, often referred to as El Arranque because of its afternoon/early-evening El Arranque milongas; Nuevo Chique in Casa de Galicia is a lovely option for those gaining in confidence; and the earlier hours of the more high-powered milongas can be the least scary.

There is another style of Traditional milonga popular with solo dancers as well as couples and groups, and these milongas are also less daunting than the high-powered places. They are usually a bit farther out of town and have a local feel, and the organisers work hard to create a friendly atmosphere. Male and female solo dancers may be seated at adjacent tables rather than in formal rows on opposite sides of the room, there are tandas when women can invite men, verbal invitations are not completely frowned upon, it's acceptable for men to walk the room to widen their cabeceo options... all can help to make these places feel more accessible to the first-timer. A local clientele can mean that dancing ability varies, so you might want to observe potential partners dancing first, but basically everyone is out to have a great time, and I love that idea. This is what I fondly think of as Traditional and very sociable tango, Argentine style, and it can be fun. Examples of milongas that fit this profile are Sueño Porteño (Wednesday) and La Milonguita (Sunday).

Comprehensive information on the Traditional venues mentioned here and the milongas held in them can be found in **7 Traditional Places to Try First**, later in **Part 3**.

What can you expect from the milongas in my Traditional category?

1.   More locals and fewer tourists than in the Tourist-circuit and Informal venues, and in some places the regular locals may prefer to dance with other regular locals.

2.   An older average age, though a few younger dancers sometimes arrive much later in the night from other venues. Rule of thumb — the earlier in the day, the older the clientele: El Arranque at 5pm on a Monday, many *jubilados* (pensioners or the retired); Cachirulo, Saturday at 3am, more of a mixed bag, but even so, not the youngest crowd.

3.   Traditional seating with men down one side, women facing them down the other, couples and groups at the ends of the room (or a

variation on this theme). In some places, like Nuevo Salón La Argentina (El Arranque), the solo dancers sit opposite each other with only a narrow aisle between them: the dance floor is further down the room. In other places, especially where the size or shape of the salón demands it (as at Sueño Porteño in Boedo Tango), the seating is more mixed to give everyone some good cabeceo options.

4.   To be seated by the host on arrival: it's completely unacceptable to march in and choose your own seat. Regulars have their 'own' tables. In some milongas, like those held in El Beso, competition for front-row seats is fierce, and you are unlikely to get a well-located seat on your first visit.

5.   An elegant and often glamorous standard of dress. In Traditional milongas, to be noticed and remembered (for the right reasons) is everything. Jeans are not worn by many, might put people off dancing with you, and could even (in a few places) be the cause of refused entry.

6.   Invitation to dance by cabeceo only, apart from in a few places, as already mentioned.

7.   Tandas of tango, milonga, vals, canyengue, tropical or Latin as a few people call it (some places), chacarera (some places) and rock 'n' roll (some places), with everyone clearing the floor between the tandas. Traditional music. No electronic tango. Pop music may be heard, but only in the cortina breaks between the tandas.

8.   Adherence to the traditional milonga códigos.

9.   Sometimes a raffle/draw with prizes of bubbly, CDs, tango shoes, or maybe even a pizza!

10. Always, a range of dancing skill, though in the most high-powered places, at least some of the crème of the traditional crème are undoubtedly present. Dance style is at the traditional end of the spectrum and is close (often very close) embrace: the style predominantly danced in these milongas is the style commonly referred to as tango milonguero (see **Styles of tango** in **Part 2**).

Five tips to help you get the best out of the most serious Traditional venues and milongas:

1.   Perform the cabeceo like a pro. You will need to know about the cabeceo (see **Cabeceo** in **Part 2**) and use it with confidence, sometimes at long distance, from one side of the dance floor to the other.
2.   Be seen to be in the know by adhering to the códigos for behaviour in the milongas. The most sought-after dancers will only dance with a stranger who looks like they know what they are doing.
3.   Follow **Rule 10: Stay late. Go back.** Stay until the final hour, return the following week. Commitment does get rewarded (eventually) by the regulars and, if you keep going back, you might become one. Arriving early can also be a good idea, as people can notice you before the crush of regulars blocks the view.
4.   Be seen to dance. If you know someone you can hit the floor with early on (perhaps someone you have met at the group class before the milonga), do so because then people will see that you can dance and be more likely to invite or accept you.
5.   Glam up, wear something memorable, and power up your magnetic energy. These places can be competitive and it's all about being noticed. Newbie wallflowers of either sex will be invisible and ignored.

The first time you visit the most high-powered Traditional milongas of Buenos Aires, you are going to have to follow **Rule 8: Be realistic.** Unless you are a supermodel of either sex, or a fabulous dancer with a dance partner to show you off at the start, you may not dance much in the Cachirulo, Lujos or El Maipú milongas the first time you visit. In these places you have to earn the right, and it's probably better to know it before you go, to avoid disappointment. I once sat for five hours in a crowded-to-bursting Saturday-night Cachirulo and danced two tandas, and much more recently I sat for two hours (in the fourth row back) and danced none — on the latter occasion, I gave up and went home. It can sometimes feel like very hard work. On the other hand it's fascinating to see these places in operation, as it's all part of the experience. Don't be too downhearted if you do not dance immediately — it's probably nothing personal, and you are definitely not alone in your plight.

Informal Venues/Milongas/Prácticas

I've slipped the word práctica in here, and this is because some Informal-category venues describe their open dance nights as prácticas, but they keep the hours of the milongas, or maybe start and end a bit earlier. These prácticas definitely feel most relaxed early in the session, immediately after the classes finish, when the dance floor is emptiest, but as the more high-powered dancers arrive and fill the floor... well, then, to be honest, I don't think there is much difference between the Informal-category public prácticas of Buenos Aires and the Informal-category milongas; though, in some of the prácticas there are no tandas, and you have to decide when to say *Gracias* and move on.

The Informal scene offers up a very different feast to the Traditional one, and it's probable that your 'tango homes' will lie mainly in one or the other. To my eyes, the Informal scene has more in common with tango in my home country: groups of friends hanging out together; a greater proportion of open-embrace tango; more verbal invitations to dance; some non-traditional music; and a less conservative vibe. This Informal scene is most popular with younger dancers, from both Buenos Aires and abroad.

In Buenos Aires tango though, Informal doesn't necessarily mean friendly or accessible, and many newcomers remark that in general this scene can be a nut that takes a bit of time and persistence to crack. From my own experience, if you turn up alone, it can feel as if everyone else has lots of mates and options for dance partners, and you don't. People tend to sit with their friends and focus inwards rather than casting their eyes around the room at new faces. Newcomers will most likely end up dancing with other newcomers at first.

But if you want to dance a more fluid-embrace style of tango, hang out with the younger crowd, dance to electronic tango or reverse traditional roles in tango, you must check out some of the Informal places.

Three well-known and popular Informal spots are La Viruta, Club Villa Malcolm (on its more informal nights) and Milonga10 in Club Fulgor. These are all in or very close to the Buenos Aires district of Palermo.

Into this category also fall two famous gay-friendly options for tango in Buenos Aires: La Marshàll on Friday and Sunday nights and Tango Queer on Tuesday night. These are open to everyone, gay or straight, and are the milongas where every variation on the theme of role reversal in tango is completely accepted, and frowned on by no-one.

If you like Informal, but don't fancy the idea of coping with the cliques, then one lovely venue is La Glorieta, best known for its Saturday and Sunday evening milongas. It's a roofed bandstand in a Belgrano park, with no seats, lots of locals, and dancers of every conceivable level and type mixing together and enjoying themselves. It's fun and it's relatively easy to invite and be invited to dance. I built my tango confidence there when I was new in town, and many first-time visitors do.

Comprehensive information on the Informal venues mentioned here and the milongas and prácticas held in them can be found in **7 Informal Places to Try First**, later in **Part 3**.

There can be some wide variations, but in general, here's what you can expect from the milongas and prácticas in my Informal category:

1. Lots of tourists who may mostly end up dancing with each other, unless they become known and respected regulars. Often the tourists know one another because they attend group classes together, and this is a good way of being sure of having a few people to dance with in some of these venues. The scene is also popular with many long-stay foreigners.
2. The younger generation, but not exclusively.
3. A mix of tango styles being danced, with a greater proportion of the open-embrace tango commonly referred to as tango nuevo, and tango salón (see **Styles of tango** in **Part 2**).
4. The younger famous tango professionals and tango teachers either performing exhibitions or out dancing socially with their friends.
5. Informal but stylish dress, including dance sneakers instead of stilettos for some.
6. Table seating or, in a few places, a row of chairs with no tables around the walls. In some venues that have table seating, such as La Viruta, you can reserve a table in advance, in others no.

7.   A relaxation of the traditional milonga códigos: sometimes music is played continuously throughout the session (most common in the prácticas), rather than in tandas separated by cortinas; verbal invitations instead of the cabeceo may be the norm, especially when the lights are low; and in a few places, the exchange of traditional roles is acceptable and women may dance with women, and men with men.

8.   Sometimes, but not as often as foreigners might be used to, a few tandas of electronic tango music.

9.   A range of dancing skills, even in places hyped as being for 'the best' dancers.

10.   On busy nights, on crowded dance floors, it's possible to be kicked above the waist, by flying heels. Do try to avoid being the culprit.

Although I've enjoyed nights out with my mates in all the Informal-category places listed in this book, I confess I have not persevered with this scene myself, basically because I quickly found out that my 'tango homes' lie more towards the Traditional end of the Buenos Aires tango spectrum. However, many of my friends have found their Happy Tango here, and here are their top five tips for settling into the Informal scene as fast as possible:

1.   Take the classes (if they are at your level) before the Informal-category milongas and prácticas. With a bit of luck you'll make a few friends to dance with when the class ends. If you're alone it can feel very intimidating to walk into these places later in the night when everyone seems to be sitting with a group. The transition from class to milonga or práctica is less scary: you are there already, you might be able to sit with people from the class, and you'll be able to choose a good seat before the crowds arrive.

2.   Take classes at the tango schools or attend the guided tango prácticas well known for attracting dancers who are likely to choose venues on the Informal scene. Try DNI if you're a fan of a more nuevo style of tango. Try the Sunderland prácticas, led by Carlos and Rosa Pérez, if you're serious about tango salón (see **Appendix A: 10 Tango Schools** for details of both).

3. Be seen dancing at your highest level. This requires that you have someone to dance with, at least in the beginning. If others see you dance, and like what they see, they may then either invite you or accept you later, or tomorrow, or next week.

4. Become a regular on this scene. Be seen night after night, at the classes, the prácticas and the milongas. As your face gets known, you'll get more dances. Follow **Rule 10: Stay Late. Go Back**.

5. Ask your dance partners and tango-class peers about the latest 'in' places. The Informal scene is perhaps the most impermanent. New milongas and prácticas pop up all the time (as others close or move home) and news is shared between friends and like-minded dancers by word of mouth. Rather than having regularly updated websites, most of the more Informal places have Facebook profiles, pages or groups, so to stay in touch you'll need a Facebook account.

And one final word on the Informal scene. Do realise that a feeling of rejection (or some variation on that theme) is inevitable and is experienced by most newbies at times: feeling invisible; resenting the cliques; wishing you were a supermodel; wishing that you were dancing with a supermodel; longing for someone, anyone, to look your way. It's true everywhere in the Buenos Aires tango scene, but perhaps more so in the Informal places, where it can sometimes feel like everyone has more dancing mates than you. But even the people sitting in the cliques had to do their time, and I'm afraid that you will have to too. Don't take any of it personally. It's just the way it is here.

20 Places to Try First

The following pages detail twenty places to dance tango in Buenos Aires. My definition of a 'place' is very loose, and is a milonga or a práctica (or a group of milongas or prácticas) held in a given venue.

My twenty places offer you the chance to experience Buenos Aires tango right across the board. There are **6 Tourist-circuit, 7 Traditional** and **7 Informal Places to Try First**. For each place, I describe the venue, along with at least one milonga or práctica held there, and tell you the stuff you need to know, including the website or Facebook profile when one is available. You can use the information to help you decide where to dance first, perhaps based on which sound like they could be your 'tango homes'.

In choosing these particular places, I'm offering you a wide selection of Buenos Aires tango, so that you can see for yourself just how varied it is. I'm not saying that these twenty places are the best in town (after all, your best might be very different to mine); nor am I saying that they are my personal favourites, though one or two of them might be; and I'm definitely not saying that you should stick with these and not dance further afield. In **Beyond the 20 with the Milonga Listings**, I'll be encouraging you to explore and discover other wonderful places for yourself, by telling you where you can find details of all the (publicised) milongas held in Buenos Aires, by day of the week.

At the time of writing, my **20 Places to Try First** are all going strong. I hope they still will be when you come to town, but I urge you to check the current month's milonga listings or the individual websites and Facebook pages before turning up at any of them. Both awareness and acceptance of the impermanence of Buenos Aires tango are essential for avoiding unnecessary disappointments en route to Happy Tango. You have been warned!

6 Tourist-circuit Places
to Try First

CONFITERÍA IDEAL

also known as La Ideal or Ideal
**Suipacha 380/4, 1st floor
(Microcentro)**

**The matinée milongas hosted
by different organisers. Try
Friday and Sunday afternoons.**

confiteriaideal.com

**Perhaps the most famous historic
tango venue in Buenos Aires, it
has been featured in many films,
including Sally Potter's *The Tango
Lesson*. The salón boasts an
impressive stained glass and cut
metalwork roof, elegant columns
and a spacious, smooth (for its
age) hard-tile dance floor.
The place has an air of faded
grandeur, though some
renovations were carried out
in 2012, and a timeless feel that
offers a precious glimpse into the
past. Its matinée milongas are
among the most accessible in the
city: newcomers are likely to be
invited/accepted for dances.**

Getting there and away
By taxi: ask for *Suipacha y Corrientes*.
When leaving, turn left and walk to the
corner with Avenida Corrientes where
plenty of taxis pass by.

More to explore
Friday and Sunday matinées are
busiest, so beginners and newbies
might prefer other quieter afternoons.
Late milongas in the Tourist-circuit
category are held most nights, and live
orchestras sometimes play: try
Unitango (Facebook **Unitango
Milongas**) on Friday.

The stuff you need to know

Dancing between the columns of La
Ideal can make you feel that you take
your tiny place in the great story of
tango argentino.

Bottom feeders can be a nuisance.
Women should think twice before
accepting verbal invitations. Men
should use the cabeceo. Everyone
should try to observe the dancers
before inviting or accepting.

Don't be surprised if someone you
dance with turns out to be a tango
teacher and hands you their business
card after the tanda.

Non-tango-dancing tourists will
probably snap pictures of you for their
holiday albums.

There is a balcony over Suipacha where
you can go for a smoke or a breath of
fresh air (when the smokers aren't in
residence). You might need a cooling
breeze, as there is no air conditioning in
this venue. In summer take a fan and
something to wipe your brow. In winter
it's chilly, so take an extra layer.

The average age of the regulars is older,
but a few younger tourists pass through
too, so be prepared for anything!

Snack food is available. Prices are
relatively high, as it is a touristic spot.

SALÓN CANNING

also known as Canning
**Scalabrini Ortiz 1331
(Palermo)**

**The Monday, Tuesday and
Friday night milongas from
11pm by Parakultural**

parakultural.com.ar

**Famous, large and stylish salón
with a high ceiling and tables
surrounding a stunning square,
polished, wooden dance floor. It
regularly offers performances by
live orchestras and tango
exhibitions by the professionals.
The Parakultural milongas have
a glamorous feel and the mixed
seating arrangement especially
suits groups of friends or solo
dancers who find rows of single-
sex seating too intimidating.**

Getting there and away
By taxi: ask for *Scalabrini Ortiz y
Cabrera*. When leaving, it's easy to get
a taxi right outside the venue.

More to explore
For an accessible Traditional-category
milonga in this venue, consider the
Wednesday matinée **A Puro Tango**
(Facebook **A Puro Tango**). It's good for
solo dancers and has a traditional
seating arrangement. It's relatively
relaxed and so is an option for
newcomers to the Traditional scene.
Older age range. A Puro Tango also
hosts milongas in Canning on
Saturday night and Sunday evening.

The stuff you need to know

The fame of the Parakultural milongas
means that they can sometimes get
overcrowded. The hordes combined
with the high percentage of tourists can
lead to problems with floorcraft; do
your bit to respect others on the dance
floor and earn the respect of the locals
in return.

Bottom feeders can be a nuisance;
ladies, think twice before accepting
verbal invitations.

The square dance floor can be difficult
to navigate, as there is a large middle
area that sucks in the inexperienced
and gets chaotic at peak times.

The room is huge, so cabeceo options
are limited to those sitting at nearby
tables. Men can walk in the aisles to
cabeceo further afield, thus the best
seats for women are those with a good
view of the length of an aisle.

The performances by live orchestras
and professional dancers don't usually
begin until at least 1.30am (normal in
Buenos Aires).

The air conditioning can be fierce, so
take a wrap or jacket.

The age range is mixed, and younger
dancers often arrive later from the
Informal-category venues.

Empanadas are available.

PORTEÑO Y BAILARÍN

also known as El Porteño or by some visiting foreigners as P and B; the venue is actually called Club Castel

Riobamba 345 (Centro)

Sunday and Tuesday night milongas from 10.30pm

Facebook: Milonga Porteño y Bailarín

Centrally located, intimate, L-shaped venue with two dance floors separated by a bar area. The floors are of hard tile. The front salón is popular with the regulars and feels a little more high-powered. The overflow of tourists and latecomers is accommodated in the back room, which has a more relaxed feel. A mixed seating arrangement results in a fairly non-intimidating vibe, and because the venue is smallish you don't have to perform long-distance cabeceos. There are sometimes performances by musicians, singers or professional dancers.

Getting there and away
By taxi: ask for *Riobamba y Corrientes*. When leaving, turn right and walk the half block to Avenida Corrientes, where it's easy to get a taxi.

The stuff you need to know

Even if you reserve, you might be seated in the back room if you are not known: any live performances usually take place in the front room, which means you will have to leave your seats and stand up to watch.

Men can move between the two rooms or stand in the bar area to widen their cabeceo options.

Women seated in one room will only get to dance with men from the other if the men walk between the two. On quieter nights when the back room is not very busy, solo-dancer women should try to get a seat in the front room.

When the front dance floor is packed, men might suggest dancing in the back room for reasons of space. Women, don't be surprised if this happens: it's nothing out of the ordinary, and he'll return you to your seat afterwards.

It can get pretty warm in this venue, especially in the back room. On summer nights, ladies should take a fan, and everyone should dress for the heat.

Mixed age range.

Some simple meals are available.

CENTRO REGIÓN LEONESA

also known as La Leonesa, Leonesa or sometimes Niño Bien, after its famous milonga
Humberto 1° 1462, 1st floor (Constitución)

The Niño Bien milonga on Thursday night from 10.30pm

Famous, historic venue with majestic staircase leading up to the spacious and elegant tango salón. The large rectangular dance floor is made of wood and is especially easy on the feet. The Niño Bien milonga has a glamorous feel and the mixed seating arrangement especially suits groups of friends or solo dancers who find rows of single-sex seating too intimidating. Couples and solo dancers may find themselves sharing a table for four with other dancers.

Getting there and away
By taxi: ask for *Humberto 1°* (1° is pronounced *primo*) *y San José*. When leaving, turn left and walk the half block to the corner with Pte. Luis S. Peña where taxis pass in the direction of the city centre: this isn't the safest of districts, so take care; it's probably best not to wait alone.

More to explore
For a Traditional-category milonga in this venue, try **La Milonga de Los Consagrados** on Saturday afternoon into evening. It offers separate seating for solo dancers, but is relatively relaxed. Older age range.

The stuff you need to know

The fame of the Niño Bien milonga means that it can sometimes get overcrowded. The hordes combined with the high percentage of tourists can lead to problems with floorcraft; do your bit to respect others on the dance floor and earn the respect of the locals in return.

Bottom feeders can be a nuisance; ladies, think twice before accepting verbal invitations.

It can be difficult to cabeceo across the dance floor once it starts filling up, but on Thursday night the seating is mixed, so everyone should have some cabeceo options nearby. Men are able to walk the room to cabeceo further afield.

There are two balconies off the entrance hall at the top of the staircase, and smokers can use these rather than heading out into the street.

The air conditioning can be inadequate in summer, so take a fan and something to wipe your brow.

Mixed age range.

Good range of food options including simple evening meals.

CLUB SUNDERLAND

also known as Sunderland
**Lugones 3161
(Villa Urquiza, making this
milonga one of the farthest
from the city centre)**

**The Saturday night La Milonga
del Mundo from 10.30pm**

sunderlandclub.com.ar

**An unusual but world-famous
venue — a cavernous basketball
court in a sports club on the edge
of Buenos Aires Capital Federal.
There is usually a performance by
professional dancers, and you
might spot a few famous tango
personalities in the crowd. It's an
example (albeit, rather a well-
known one) of a Saturday night
social milonga (of the type often
referred to by Argentines as a _club
de barrio_ or a _milonga de barrio_)
attended by groups of friends and
couples from the _barrio_ (district)
where the venue is located. Solo
dancers, go in a group so that you
can dance with each other, in case
other options are limited.**

Getting there and away
By taxi: ask for _Lugones y Quesada por
Avenida Congreso_. When leaving, the
best bet for a taxi will be Avenida
Congreso, but there won't be many taxis
operating this far out of town late at
night, so it could be best to ask the Club
staff to call one for you.

The stuff you need to know

All may not be lost if you are a solo
dancer. Men can walk around the venue
and look out for groups of tourists or
groups of women, where the women are
wearing tango shoes and look as if they
are actively trying to find dance
partners; don't waste your time seeking
dances from groups of Argentines who
look as if they are having a night out
with friends or family because they will
most likely dance only with each other
or with people they know. Women
should keep their eye out for men who
are walking the room in this way.

Hard-tile floor, which can be tough on
the feet.

Can be chilly in the cooler seasons
because it is such a vast space, so do
take an extra layer.

The age range is mixed, but weighted
towards the older end of the spectrum.

Good range of food options, you can eat
a full evening meal, and having dinner
together will be a part of the night out
for many Argentines.

If you are British, do go and see the
Sunderland football shirt on display in
the front bar: it's a tiny connection with
your homeland!

PLAZA DORREGO

Humberto 1° 449, at the corner with Anselmo Aieta (San Telmo)

Milonga Placita del Pañuelo Blanco, outdoors on Sunday evenings from around 8pm

Facebook: Milonga Placita del pañuelo Blanco

A chance to dance under the stars (weather permitting) in a relaxed atmosphere. You will, almost certainly, be surrounded by interested-spectator tourists (who sometimes applaud politely at the end of each tanda) because the milonga takes place as the hugely popular San Telmo Sunday market draws to a close. If you don't mind a non-dancing audience, it's a laid-back outdoor venue that attracts a wide range of dancers.

Getting there and away

You could check out the colourful market along Defensa street and in Plaza Dorrego in the afternoon and stay on for the milonga. Alternatively, from the city centre by taxi, ask for *Bolivar y Humberto 1°*, then walk the half block along Humberto 1° to Plaza Dorrego. When leaving, catch a taxi heading towards the city centre along Defensa (the one-way street at the higher end of Plaza Dorrego). Adjust your level of alertness as you move away from the busy scene of the milonga; the quieter streets in this area can feel on the edgy side after dark.

The stuff you need to know

It's in a touristic spot and there are many non-tango people milling around. There is nowhere to leave your stuff, so best to go in your dance shoes and keep any valuables on your person or leave them at home. Some dance with their bags hanging over their shoulders.

Go prepared to stand around the edge or to sit on the surrounding walls because any tables near to the dance floor belong to the nearby restaurants; alternatively if you're hungry and you've got the cash, grab a front-row table and treat yourself to a slap-up meal, with a great view of the dancers. When I last visited, the dinner tables were gone from beside the dance floor, though that may have been a temporary change.

The dance floor is a temporary and well-worn (slightly rubbery) affair rolled out over the plaza, and although it works well enough, heels can catch in the joins and at times you might find yourself dancing off the mat and on to stone. For this reason, many women dance in flat shoes at this milonga.

There's a friendly vibe and the men wander around and invite the women to dance. You can expect a range of dance styles and levels.

There's no entry fee. A hat is passed round for contributions.

Mixed age range.

7 Traditional Places
to Try First

NUEVO SALÓN LA ARGENTINA

also known as El Arranque, after its popular matinée milongas
Bartolomé Mitre 1759 (Congreso/Centro)

The El Arranque matinée milongas held afternoon into evening on Monday, Tuesday, Thursday and Saturday from 3pm

Mostly frequented by the older generation, the El Arranque matinée milongas offer a non-intimidating opportunity to dip your toe into the more Traditional milonga scene and practise your cabeceo technique. Solo dancers are seated facing each other across an aisle (tables of men mixed in with tables of women): good, because the dancers don't block your view of potential partners. Couples are seated down the sides of the large dance floor, which is of hard tile. The venue is centrally located, but some might feel it lacks atmosphere as the room is a bit stark and lit with bright lights overhead.

Getting there and away
By taxi: ask for *Bartolomé Mitre y Callao*. When leaving, catch a taxi on Bartolomé Mitre, or turn right and walk the half block to the corner with Avenida Callao where it's easy to get a taxi (and where there will usually be plenty of people around).

The stuff you need to know

One of the only places (perhaps the only place) remaining in the Centro that offers differential entry fees for women and men, the entrada for women is lower than that for men.

It's relatively easy for newcomers to get dances at the El Arranque matinée milongas as they are at the less high-powered and more relaxed end of the city-centre Traditional tango spectrum.

The dance floor is located at one end of the room, so it can be difficult to observe the dancers, but do try: there is likely to be a wide range of dance levels and occasionally bottom feeders can be a nuisance too.

Because the seating is to one side, both man and woman have to stand and meet each other on the dance floor, as the man probably won't walk to the woman's table. Women, stay seated as long as possible to make sure that you are the chosen one: hold his eyes with yours if you can, and perhaps wait for another signal from him, once he has reached the dance floor, that he is waiting for you. It's a bit tricky, but you'll manage it.

An older clientele.

Snack food is available.

EL BESO

Riobamba 416, 1st floor (Centro)

elbesotangobar.com.ar

If you fancy the more high-powered Traditional scene, try Cachirulo on Tuesday from 8pm or Lujos on Thursday from 6.30pm.

A famous, centrally located venue, known for its generally high standard of dancing. The venue is small and has either an intimate or a claustrophobic feel, depending on how you view it. The dance floor is of smooth wood. The seating arrangements are traditional, with separate areas for male solo dancers, female solo dancers and couples. The venue isn't suitable for large groups because the tables seat up to four and are arranged in rows around the dance floor. This is a venue for those who are confident using the cabeceo or who are prepared to learn fast: the milonga códigos are respected, and competition for the most popular dancers is fierce.

Getting there and away
By taxi: ask for *Riobamba y Corrientes*. When leaving, turn right and walk the few steps to the corner with Avenida Corrientes where it's easy to get a taxi.

More to explore
Well-established Traditional-category milongas are also held in this venue on Saturday and Sunday nights.
La Marshàll offers a more Informal style on a Friday night.

The stuff you need to know

The Cachirulo and Lujos milongas are very popular, as are all the El Beso milongas: unless you are a regular it's important for solo dancers to arrive early to get the best available seats.

The small size of the venue and the packed-in seats mean that it isn't easy to walk around unobtrusively once you have sat down. Men can go and stand in the bar area to widen their cabeceo options a little.

When it's busy, you need to perform the cabeceo fast at the start of a tanda before the dancing couples block your view of seated potential partners. Seats with a clear view of the bar area are favoured by some women, because if you're seated close to the bar, you can still find the eyes of male dancers standing at the bar, once the tanda has begun.

Because the seats are very close together, it's easy to make mistakes with the cabeceo. Follow the tips in the entry **Cabeceo** in **Part 2** to avoid unnecessary embarrassment.

Mixed age range.

Variety of food options, but the lack of space and somewhat competitive ambience don't exactly make for a relaxed dinner out. Might be best to focus on dancing.

CASA DE GALICIA

also known as Chiqué, after its Nuevo Chiqué milongas
San José 224, 1st floor (Monserrat)

The Nuevo Chiqué matinée milongas held on Tuesday and Thursday from 4pm

Facebook: **Nuevochique Milonga del Corazon**

Centrally located, atmospheric, mid-sized salón with a lovely wooden dance floor and fabulous old paintings around the walls. Traditional seating arrangement, with men on one side, women on the other and couples and small groups at the ends. A great place to practise your cabeceo technique in a milonga with an authentic vibe, where the códigos are respected by everyone, but where the atmosphere is relatively relaxed and not too intimidating.

Getting there and away
By taxi: ask for *San José y Alsina*. When leaving, turn right and walk the two and a half blocks to Avenida de Mayo, where taxis should be plentiful; stay alert as you walk, because the side streets in this area can feel on the edgy side after dark (though in summer you might be leaving in daylight hours).

More to explore
The Traditional-style milonga **El Maipú de Lucy y Dany** is held on Friday evening in this venue.

The stuff you need to know

Can be slightly tricky to cabeceo directly across the dance floor once dancing starts in earnest, so you have to be quick at the start of the tanda.

Great seats for women are along the side wall, but nearer to the entrance end of the room, as some solo male dancers sit at the front of this end section and others stand there from time to time to widen their cabeceo options. Also good for women are the seats at the front of this entrance-end section as it is in very clear view of the male dancers seated down the side of the room.

Men can stand at the end of the room near the entrance to temporarily widen their cabeceo options – this can be done, without drawing too much attention, on the way back in from a trip to the baños.

One of my favourite milonga bathrooms is located on the way in, for ladies to change their shoes and powder their noses. It has a wonderful attendant in charge of proceedings and all kinds of useful items on hand.

Good snack food available, including a tasty and often home-made *torta* (cake) option which goes great with a late afternoon pick-me-up coffee.

There is a Spanish restaurant on the second floor of Casa de Galicia, Rias Baixas Restaurante, which is said to be excellent (though untried by me), so you could eat there after the milonga.

An older clientele.

CLUB GRICEL

also known as Gricel
La Rioja 1180
(San Cristóbal)

clubgriceltango.com.ar

At the more Tourist-circuit (accessible to newcomers) end of the spectrum, the Monday night milonga Lunes de Tango from 9pm

A famous historic venue with an intimate feel, despite being fairly large: the golden-coloured dance floor, columns and low ceilings all contribute to the cosy atmosphere. Perhaps the most photographed feature is the pink neon Club Gricel sign above the bar. Gricel is a Traditional venue and on quieter nights it has a lovely authentic feel. But in the high tourist season, it can be packed with visitors from abroad. Be prepared for a crush, and stay late to beat the crowds.

Getting there and away
By taxi: ask for *Rioja y San Juan*. When leaving, either get a taxi on Rioja or turn left and walk the half block to the corner with Avenida San Juan where plenty of taxis pass: this isn't the safest of districts, so take care; it's probably best not to wait alone.

More to explore
For other milongas in Gricel, try the Thursday evening milonga **La Cachila**, known to be a relatively friendly option for solo dancers. Older age range.

The stuff you need to know

The fame of Gricel, especially on a Monday night, means that it can sometimes get hectic. The hordes combined with the high percentage of tourists can lead to problems with floorcraft; do your bit to respect others on the dance floor.

Bottom feeders can be a nuisance; ladies, think twice before accepting verbal invitations.

Women are perhaps best seated down the sides of the room or at the end nearest the bar, as these areas are most active, with plenty of men walking around. The end of the room near the door always feels lower in energy to me, is often populated by groups of friends, and when I sit near there, I don't attract as many lovely dances. It's less important for men, as they can walk down the aisles to widen their options.

The dance floor is beautiful, but ageing, resulting in a slight corrugation of the wood: it's possible to catch stiletto heels in the cracks. But on the upside, it feels soft and springy and is wonderfully easy on the feet.

An older clientele, though the range of tourists mixes it up a bit.

Good food options, including full evening meals.

LA NACIONAL

Alsina 1465, 1st floor (Monserrat)

lanacionaltango.com

El Maipú de Lucy y Dany:
Monday from 6pm

Yira Yira:
Friday from 10.30pm

JL en La Nacional:
Saturday from 8pm

La Nacional milongas are held in a historic tango salón upstairs in the quite lovely building that is the Asociazione Nazionale Italiana. The stairs with their minstrels' gallery midway up create a very special path to the ticket desk. These are extremely popular milongas, especially loved by solo dancers who come to dance every week with their favourite partners. The codigos are respected and observed, the dance floor can get busy mid-session and there is serious competition for the best dancers.

Getting there and away

By taxi: ask for *San José y Alsina*. When leaving, get a taxi in the street outside or turn right and walk the half block to the corner with Pte. Luis S. Peña where taxis pass in the direction of the city centre. It can feel a little edgy in this area, so stay alert as you walk or wait.

More to explore

El Maipú de Lucy y Dany is also held on Friday evening in Casa de Galicia.

The stuff you need to know

Each of the milongas in this venue has a different organiser and character, and the table layouts and seating arrangements vary. In all cases reservations are a good idea, and on arrival you should wait just inside the door to be seated by the host.

The moment you walk in to the salón you are 'on view' from the seats just inside the door, so it's a good idea to leave coats at the coat check and change shoes in the restrooms before entering.

The room is long and narrowish, so long-distance cabeceos may be needed. This requires a bit of confidence and a good technique: follow the tips in the entry **Cabeceo** in **Part 2** to avoid awkward situations.

This venue doesn't allow for too much unobtrusive walking around. Men can linger briefly on their way in from a trip to the baños, but they might find themselves blocking the waitresses or the hosts. Most stay seated.

The floor can be quite slippery as it's very smooth wood, so be aware as you step out for the first time.

Fierce air conditioning, welcome on hot days but can feel a little chilly.

Age range mixed, but generally on the older side.

A good range of food options. For a snack try the *empanada caprese* (small open pastry filled with cheese, tomato and fresh basil).

BOEDO TANGO

also known as Boedo
**San Juan 3330, 1st floor
(Boedo)**

**The Sueño Porteño milongas
on Wednesday from 7pm,
Friday from 10pm and Sunday
from 6pm**

**clubdetango.blogia.com
Facebook: Sueño Porteño**

Intriguing venue above a
supermarket, with two wooden
dance floors (adjoining but with a
somewhat unusual step between).
No reservations are taken and so
it's a case of first come, first
served for the best seats, which
are perhaps around the larger of
the dance floors. The Sueño
Porteño milongas have a local
vibe and a friendly, relaxed feel.
Good for groups, couples and solo
dancers... a fun night out for
everyone. Live orchestras
sometimes play, and the milongas
occasionally have themed dress
codes suggested, but they are not
compulsory! Join the Facebook
group to stay on top of the Sueño
Porteño programme.

Getting there and away
By taxi: ask for *San Juan y Virrey
Liniers*. When leaving, it's easy to get a
taxi right outside the venue on Avenida
San Juan. This isn't the safest of
districts after dark, so take care; it's
best to wait directly outside the venue
on the main avenida.

The stuff you need to know

The unusual layout, around a central
stairwell, means that wherever you sit,
you can only see part of the venue. Men
have to walk the room to widen their
cabeceo options. Ladies, look up and
interested and the guys will find you,
though you may want to be selective
and practise your 'look away, not just
now' technique, and the occasional
verbal *No por ahora, gracias* may
be needed.

Because of the layout, it's impossible for
women to observe all the dancers from
their seats. This is a venue where you
are forced to take a few chances. The
level of dancing is mixed, but people are
out to enjoy themselves and I think you
have to go with that attitude too and be
prepared for anything.

You'll hear a few announcements at the
Sueño Porteño milongas. For example,
there is sometimes a tanda where men
can invite women to dance by handing
them a rose, or a tanda when women
can invite men by offering them a sweet
or a chocolate from a big bowl placed on
a chair in the centre of the dance floor,
and there's usually a show, a high-
energy tanda of chacarera... and so on.
This is a local milonga and the
organiser does her best to make it
friendly and fun. I think she succeeds.
If your preference is for a more formal
Traditional scene or a very high-
powered, competitive scene, then this
one might not be for you.

An older clientele.

There is a separate restaurant area,
though you can also eat at your milonga
table and the food is good.

PLAZA BOHEMIA

also known by its address
Alsina 2540
(Once)

plazabohemia.net

**The Lujos milonga on
Sunday from 6.30pm is the
most well known in this venue.**

**Pleasant, mid-sized venue with a
square dance floor surrounded
by a fairly spacious arrangement
of tables. The location is gaining
in popularity since becoming
home to the much-loved Lujos
milonga which relocated here
from Plaza Bohemia's previous
home at Maipú 444 (no longer
a tango spot).**

**From the street, you enter down a
long corridor with the restrooms
on the left after a small open
courtyard with seating for a chat
or a shoe change; keep going to
the very end where wonderfully
air-conditioned tango awaits you.**

Getting there and away
By taxi: ask for *Alsina entre Alberti y
Saavedra*. When leaving, get a taxi
outside the venue on Alsina or you can
turn right, then left on Alberti and walk
the two blocks to Avenida Rivadavia
where taxis should be plentiful. This is
not the safest district, especially after
dark, so if you're alone it may be best
to wait at the door for a taxi.

More to explore
See the venue website for other dance
events in Plaza Bohemia, as they are
steadily increasing in number. Friday's
La Milonga de Elsita or Tuesday's
Derecho Viejo are two possibilities.

The stuff you need to know

The coat check and payment point is
inside the salón, on the left just after
you enter.

Lujos (same organisers as Lujos in
El Beso, Thursdays) is a milonga where
the more traditional códigos are
respected by everyone.

The dance floor seems to me to be
laminate, and is pretty hard under foot,
so be prepared to pace yourself if you
are sensitive to non-sprung surfaces. It
also slopes slightly, downwards towards
the entrance.

The medium size, square shape and
relatively bright lighting of the room
make the cabeceo fairly easy to
perform; everyone has possibilities,
though those with a good and confident
long-distance technique will do best.

The place is spacious enough for a
degree of movement around the room
for men wishing to widen their cabeceo
options, particularly in the largest part
of the salón where both the entrance
and bar are located.

This is a great venue in the summer
months when the city suffers forty
degree temperatures, because the
air conditioning is top notch.
Conversely, if you're not a fan of
chills, take an extra layer.

Older age range.

Good menu.

7 Informal Places to Try First

LA VIRUTA

also known as Viruta or La Viru
Armenia 1366
(Palermo)

The weekend *bailes* (dance events) on Friday and Saturday nights, from around midnight through to 6am (the latest running in the city) — you really can dance right through until morning — organised by

lavirutatango.com

Popular, large, low-ceilinged, basement venue that feels more like a club than a milonga. It offers loud surround-sound-style music, semi-darkness and a very relaxed and slightly scruffy vibe. The dance floor is of hard tile. There are regular performances by live orchestras, and dance exhibitions; see the website for the programme.

Getting there and away
By taxi: ask for *Armenia y Cabrera*. When leaving, lots of taxis queue up outside in Armenia street. Or turn right and walk the half block to the corner with Niceto Vega, where taxis pass in the direction of the city centre; usually there are other people leaving/waiting, so it feels relatively safe whatever the hour.

More to explore
La Viruta hosts prácticas on Wednesday, Thursday and Sunday nights too, though there might be more electronic tango, there's no *medialunas* breakfast, and dancing finishes earlier.

The stuff you need to know

Straight after the classes finish, there are a lot of beginners and improvers on the dance floor. The higher calibre dancers arrive later when other venues close, mostly after 3.30am when the entry fee is waived.

Tandas of music genres such as rock 'n' roll, cumbia, salsa and even disco are mixed with the tango tandas earlier in the night, with the proportion of tango increasing from around 2.30am — another reason why the more experienced tango dancers arrive in the early hours of the morning.

The mix of dance levels (at times, beginners mixed in with professionals) and the crowds at peak times can result in a chaotic dance floor.

There are tandas on Fridays and Saturdays, but they can be long, at up to six tangos, so do choose your partners wisely.

Some say it's a bit of a pick-up joint. Verbal invitations to dance are the norm because of the informality and the dim lighting, so ladies will have to use their judgement. It's a good place to go with a few friends.

Mixed age range; you'll see it all, if you do the whole session.

Full meals available earlier in the night. On Friday and Saturday nights, fresh *medialunas* (croissants) arrive around 4.15am, usually during the chacarera tanda. Stay for breakfast!

CLUB VILLA MALCOLM

also known as Malcolm
Córdoba 5064 (Palermo)

The El Motivo práctica on Monday from 10pm:
elmotivotango.com

The Fruto Dulce milonga on Wednesday from 10.30pm:
frutodulcetangos.blogspot.com.ar

The Tangocool práctica on Friday from 11.30pm:
tangocool.com

This venue, behind the club's informal café/restaurant, slightly resembles a school hall, but strings of coloured lights and semi-darkness can turn it into a place with a cool-party vibe. These three dance events (by different organisers) are held after popular tango classes. The Villa Malcolm prácticas are firm favourites with dancers of less traditional styles of tango. The floor is of hard tile. Regular exhibitions by the famous.

Getting there and away
By taxi: ask for *Córdoba y Thames* (pronounced Tam-ez, with the stress on the Tam!). When leaving, it's easy to get a taxi on Avenida Córdoba, but it'll have to turn to head back to the city centre.

More to explore
For more milongas here, try **Soho Tango (sohotango.blogspot.com)** on Thursday and the very traditional (códigos enforced) **Cachirulo** on Saturday.

The stuff you need to know

Character varies according to the organiser, but these three events are loved by the younger, innovative crowd.

If there's a class at your dance level before the práctica/milonga (check the websites of the individual organisers for details), do it and meet a few people to dance with after the class.

The majority of the seating is to one side of the dance floor in what feels like an adjoining room. Solo men tend to walk around this more open area and also stand between the entrance and the dance floor, so women sitting near there might have a better chance of getting noticed. You can also keep an eye on who's arriving.

Definitely good to go with a friend, or hook up with people you know from group classes. Once the large groups of friends settle in, it can feel a bit lonely if you are on your own.

If you struggle to get dances, look for fellow tourists who might be in the same boat.

Verbal invitations and the cabeceo are both acceptable. If there are no tanda breaks, be prepared to decide when to say *Gracias* and move on.

Younger age range, but not exclusively.

Decent range of food options cooked up by the café/restaurant at the front of the venue.

LA CATEDRAL

also known as La Kte
(pronounced La Cat-ay)
**Sarmiento 4006, 1st floor
(Almagro)**

**Open every night, 8pm till late
with classes before the dancing**

lacatedralclub.com

For lovers of the word bohemian,
this is the venue to try. It's a huge
semi-renovated warehouse space
that was originally built around
1880 (the website has photos and
the history). Lighting is low,
there's an arty vibe, and the place
is popular with young Argentines
as well as foreigners, and tango
dancers and non-tango dancers
alike. It's a relaxed place to hang
out with friends. The food is
vegetarian and there's often live
music to chill out to. Classes are
held every day before the dancing
starts. Find the full programme
on the website.

The popular (especially with the
younger generation and those
wishing to learn both roles)
La Maria prácticas are held in La
Catedral on Monday and
Wednesday, though days can vary
through the year, so for details
see lamariatango.blogspot.com.ar

Getting there and away
By taxi: ask for *Sarmiento y Medrano*.
When leaving, get a taxi on this corner;
this isn't the safest of districts after
dark, so perhaps best not to
wait/walk alone.

The stuff you need to know

This is a venue perfectly suited to a
night out with your partner, a friend or
a group, whether you dance tango or
not. If you're on your own and want to
dance, do one of the classes and maybe
meet a few people to dance with later.

La Catedral is a good place for
beginners to practise together before
the place gets too hectic and the more
accomplished dancers arrive.

The dance floor is of ageing wood and
has some significant potholes, so ladies
might want to take a pair of flats; it's
quite the norm for women to dance in
practice shoes on this floor.

Verbal invitations to dance are normal,
though you can use the cabeceo too, if
there's enough light.

The furniture is a mix of sofas,
armchairs and wooden stools (that can
ravage delicate fabrics, so ladies, avoid
stockings or tights), and very different
to the table arrangements at most other
tango venues. You can't reserve, so if
you're not taking one of the classes,
you'll need to get there from 11pm to get
a decent seat.

The super-high ceiling means it's hot in
summer and chilly in winter.

Taking photos of the inside of the venue
is not encouraged.

Attracts a younger age range, though
not exclusively.

Good vegetarian food options at
reasonable prices.

CLUB FULGOR

Loyola 828
(Villa Crespo)

Milonga10 on Tuesday and Saturday night from around 10 or 11pm depending on when the classes finish

Facebook: Milonga10 and Praktika8 – Milonga10

Small, intimate, social-club venue adopted by the younger generation for these popular, high-energy dance events. Great surround-sound acoustics. Possibly not for those who suffer from claustrophobia, as when busy it can feel hemmed in and overwhelming; there is no space to move around. Known for a high standard of dancing and for hosting exhibitions by the famous.

Getting there and away
By taxi: ask for *Loyola y Thames*. When leaving, turn right and walk the half block to Serrano street for a taxi going back into the centre of Palermo. Or walk in the direction of the traffic down Serrano until you reach Avenida Córdoba where taxis will pass, though they'll need to turn to head back to the city centre. It's probably best not to wait/walk alone.

More to explore
For a Traditional-category milonga in Club Fulgor, couples could try Thursday or Sunday nights. Older age range.

The stuff you need to know

Get there early. There are no reservations and by around midnight the place can get full to bursting, with standing room only. The host doesn't seat you here; you find your own spot. Take a jacket or outer layer to leave on your seat when you get up to dance, because when it's jammed with people, you could find that your seat gets taken while you are dancing.

If the class beforehand is at your level, do it and so meet some people who might invite or accept you when the dancing starts.

The dance floor is small and gets absolutely packed, so although the place might attract some dancers who like to dance a more open-embrace style of tango, it's not always possible to do it at peak times. Get there early or stay very late, if you need space.

The dance floor is of hard tile and the type that can feel a bit sticky, especially when it's a humid night. Leather-soled dance shoes will be best, or take some talc with you.

Verbal invitations and the cabeceo are both acceptable, though it may not be easy (some say it's impossible) to get dances on your first visit(s). Go with friends if you can so you've got someone to dance with. If you're a couple, you can always visit for the experience and dance with each other.

Snack food available.

BUENOS AYRES CLUB

also known as Perú 571
**Perú 571, 1st floor
(San Telmo)**
buenosayresclub.com
Facebook: **Buenos Ayres Club**

**Bendita Milonga on Monday
night and Maldita Milonga on
Wednesday from 10.30pm**

elafronte.com.ar

Smallish venue with a non-intimidating bohemian vibe: low lighting, an ageing wooden dance floor, and slightly shabby San Telmo-style charm. There is live music every week from the popular Orquesta Típica El Afronte. They play up on the venue's stage, giving everyone a great view and the chance to dance to a contemporary tango orchestra complete with singer. When the Orquesta Típica El Afronte is on tour, there may be a substitute.

Getting there and away
By taxi: ask for *Perú y Venezuela*. When leaving, get a taxi on Perú or turn left and walk the one and a half blocks to Avenida Belgrano. Take care, as the streets in this area can feel on the edgy side after dark; it's probably best not to wait/walk alone.

More to explore
The Informal-category gay-friendly milonga by **Tango Queer** (**tangoqueer.com**) is held in this venue on a Tuesday night and also has a relaxed, non-intimidating vibe.

The stuff you need to know

Bendita and Maldita Milongas are a popular place for groups of friends to enjoy a relaxed night out watching live music. After the orchestra has performed, there is more space to dance and more opportunity because only the harder-core dancers stay on. There are some solo dancers, but it might be best to go with a friend.

The dance floor is worn, with a few holes and cracks. Stilettos can get caught, so lower heels may suit this venue; many women dance in flats and it's not frowned upon if you do.

The venue can get very chilly in winter, so do take extra layers.

Both the cabeceo and verbal invitations are acceptable; the cabeceo isn't much used here, in part because there are few solo dancers, and in part because of the informality and the low lighting.

Younger age range, though the tourists who come to see the orchestra mix it up a bit.

Empanadas are available.

The venue is especially known for its milongas featuring live orchestras, keep an eye on the venue website for what's on; on Sunday the **Milonga Andariega** is home to Orquesta Típica Andariega (**andariegatango.com.ar** and Facebook **Orquesta Típica Andariega**), and one-off concerts are also held on many Fridays and Saturdays.

LA MARSHÀLL

(gay-friendly)
in EL BESO
Riobamba 416, 1st floor
(Centro)

The La Marshàll milonga on
Friday night from 11.30pm

lamarshallmilonga.com.ar

La Marshàll welcomes everyone, including all who want to swap traditional dance roles (lead rather than follow or follow rather than lead): men can dance with men, women with women, and mixed-sex dance couples can exchange leader and follower roles in their tango, or dance the usual roles.

For details of the venue El Beso see page 139.

Getting there and away
By taxi: ask for *Riobamba y Corrientes*. When leaving, turn right and walk the few steps to the corner with Avenida Corrientes where it's easy to get a taxi.

More to explore
The La Marshàll práctica (billed as 'like the milonga but more intimate') is in Aires Tangueros at Rivadavia 1392 from 9.30pm on Sunday night. Since the first edition of *Happy Tango*, La Marshàll has moved home and night a few times; keep up to date with the latest news via their Facebook page. For Traditional-category milongas in El Beso, see **7 Traditional Places to Try First**.

The stuff you need to know

If you are going to La Marshàll for the first time and you don't know anyone, definitely consider taking the class before the milonga. It's a good way to meet a few people to dance with when the milonga begins.

If you don't want to do the class, you might feel more comfortable going to La Marshàll with a few friends. If you're a couple and just want to dance with each other, no problem; sit together, dance together and enjoy watching the other dancers exchange dance roles.

The higher calibre dancers tend to arrive later in the night. The hour immediately following the class is a great time to practise dancing in a new dance role: then the atmosphere is at its most relaxed, there is space on the dance floor, and it's acceptable to be trying out what you have learned.

Be prepared to be asked to dance either by a man or a woman, and you can then say which role you would prefer to dance (leader or follower).

Wide range of music: popular tracks and electronic tango as well as the more traditional stuff.

Mixed age range.

LA GLORIETA

**On the corner of
11 de Septiembre y
Echeverría
(Belgrano)**

**Saturday and Sunday evening
milongas from 7pm, held in a
roofed bandstand in the
Barrancas de Belgrano park**

glorietadebelgrano.com.ar

**Beautiful and unusual outdoor
venue, used in all weathers,
unless it's raining heavily. You
can mix with locals out to dance
socially in an Informal and
relatively friendly atmosphere.
It's not all Comme il Faut stilettos
here; dance in your coat and
zapatillas in winter if you want.
There are no seats: everyone just
stands around the edge of the
dance floor or sits on the railings.
No entry fee; a hat is passed later.**

Getting there and away
Arrive by the *Subte* (Subway) Line D
to Juramento, walk down Juramento,
cross through the small park with its
weekend market to Echeverría and
continue down Echeverría until you
reach the Barrancas de Belgrano park.
Find La Glorieta on the right as you
turn the corner. When leaving, get a
taxi on Echeverría or walk down to
Avenida Virrey Vertiz (the main avenue
below the park) where it's easy to get a
taxi on the park side of the road,
headed towards the city centre.

The stuff you need to know

There's nowhere safe to leave valuables:
hang your shoe bags on the inside of the
bandstand at the back, where there is
some netting put up around the railings
for protection.

Arrive early if you want space on the
dance floor, as it can get packed later.
The dance floor is circular and can
present a few challenges for those not
used to the crush.

Wide range of ages, levels and styles.
It's tricky to observe and remember
potential partners because no-one goes
back to a fixed seat, so it's a place to
take a few chances.

Men, invite women standing nearby or
walk around the standing circle to find
partners and invite verbally with a
Bailás? Or try a smile and an incline of
the head. Women, look at the men
walking past and make eye contact with
them to be invited to dance.

In spring, summer and autumn, spray
yourself with mosquito repellent or risk
getting bitten, especially around dusk.

No toilets or refreshments.

La Glorieta is a stone's throw from
Barrio Chino (the small Chinatown of
Buenos Aires), so you could head there
(Arribeños between Juramento and
Mendoza) for a Chinese meal after the
milonga. If you fancy tea and cake
beforehand, try one of my favourites —
BuddhaBA (**buddhaba.com.ar**) at
Arribeños 2288.

Beyond the 20 with the Milonga Listings

You're already off to a flying start in tango Buenos Aires. You know more than twenty places where you can dance and you have an idea of what they might offer. If you were here three weeks and you tried a different one every night, you'd still have some left over to try next time!

It's not that simple though, is it? I know that you'll want to explore beyond the twenty-plus places I've suggested. There are some great listings that you can use to find out the comprehensive lowdown on most of the milongas and prácticas in the city. They don't necessarily offer exactly the same selection, so if you want to really do your research, you'll have to check them all out. The majority are available online, so you can take a look before arriving in Buenos Aires. They all include telephone numbers for reservations (the telephone number might be for the venue, but it's often the mobile phone number of the organiser; as these can change fast, I don't include them in this book).

Even the most professionally put together listings can become out of date overnight if a milonga closes its doors, or changes hands, or becomes more (or less) popular than it once was. Check a couple of sources or make a phone call before setting out, if in any doubt. The Facebook social network is also an increasingly popular place for Buenos Aires tango organisers to post the latest on their events, especially in the case of the Informal-category prácticas and milongas: if you want to stay on top of things, you'll have to get well connected there too, because these days there can be more information about the programme on a Facebook page than on the original website.

The Listings

- **The Caserón Porteño Tango Map Guide** (select English, then Tango Map, at the website **caseronporteno.com** — Cinthia and Daniel who produce the Tango Map Guide also run the Caserón Porteño Tango Guest House and the Tango Lodge Apart-Hotel)

This is the one must-have item for every foreign tango dancer arriving in Buenos Aires. The Guide is a pamphlet listing the majority of the venues, milongas and prácticas of Buenos Aires by day of the week, with addresses and telephone numbers. Each venue is given an identifying number, and these numbers are used to mark the venues in red circles on the accompanying Tango Map (all venues are marked, but not all are listed on the map itself — the full listings are in the Guide). It's updated every two months and can be picked up free in most tango shoe stores and in some milongas. A copy of the Guide and the Tango Map, split into North and South areas of the city, can be downloaded in PDF for online viewing and printing (be aware that the online copy may not be the most recent version, and that when laid next to any other map of Buenos Aires, the Caserón Porteño Map appears 'upside down', showing the river at the bottom rather than at the top of the page, though I have never found that to be a problem).

- **The tango magazines**

There are several excellent Buenos Aires tango magazines. They are free of charge, published monthly, bimonthly or quarterly and are available in the milongas and from some tango shoe shops. They contain milonga listings, práctica listings, class listings and teacher listings. Even the advertisements contain a wealth of information, as many tango schools and teachers publicise their classes this way.

La Milonga argentina (lamilongaargentina.com.ar) is a glossy tango magazine, published monthly, with articles translated into English, offering comprehensive monthly milonga and práctica listings, including the dates when live orchestras will be playing in some venues.

el tangauta (eltangauta.com) is another very popular glossy tango magazine, published monthly. It too has articles translated into English and a full set of listings, and many tango schools advertise in its pages.

B.A. TANGO (Facebook **B.A.Tango**) is a pocket-sized glossy tango magazine, published four times a year, containing comprehensive listings. Articles are translated into English. There's no website, but the magazine can be subscribed to (in PDF), by emailing **abatango@yahoo.com** with the word 'subscription' in the subject.

PUNTO TANGO (puntotango.com.ar) is pocket-sized, has good listings and the listings on the website are regularly updated.

LOS MEJORES (revistalosmejores.com.ar) is the smallest magazine of them all, though it still has a selection of milongas listed.

DIOSTANGO (photos at **picasaweb.com/tangoguille**) is a pocket-sized tango magazine with the editor's selection in its listings.

11 More Places to Explore

The only problem you face as you begin to explore is that the listings don't tell you if a particular place is at the Traditional or the Informal end of the spectrum. So, to help you get started, here are eleven more venues, milongas and prácticas from the listings, slotted into these two categories. I'll give you the name of each milonga/práctica and its venue, and you can use the listings combined with **The Week at a Glance** (coming up at the end of **Part 3**) to do the rest. Bear in mind that some of these are fairly new, so perhaps the most likely places to experience change as time passes. So check current sources before setting out. Happy exploring!

Traditional:

- The Celia milongas at Lo de Celia Tango Club (Facebook **Lo De Celia Tango**) in Constitución. Older age range, popular with solo dancers.
- The Friday night La Baldosa (Facebook **Milonga la Baldosa**) at Salón El Pial in Flores, further out of town. Better for groups and couples than for solo dancers. Decent food, quality exhibitions, and popular with tango champions (past, present and future).
- La Piccola Milonga (Facebook **La Piccola Milonga**) on Wednesday at Aires Tangueros, Rivadavia 1392 — popular with solo dancers and small groups of friends. This intimate and attractive venue has had

several incarnations over the years and the latest is Aires Tangueros, offering classes, prácticas and milongas. Call in for the programme.

- La Milonguita (**milonguitabaile.com.ar**) re-opened its Sunday night milonga in Centro Montañés (which was closed to tango for a while) in September 2012. It also has a Wednesday evening milonga at the lovely Sala Siranush in Palermo, opposite La Viruta.
- The Friday milonga in the historic Club Sin Rumbo in the barrio of Saavedra (Facebook **Sin Rumbo "La catedral del tango"**). Famous venue, on the edge of Buenos Aires Capital Federal, beyond Villa Urquiza and Villa Pueyrredón; explore it as a couple or with friends.

Informal:

- The prácticas at Cochabamba 444 in San Telmo: try Los Jueves de Ana Postigo (Facebook **Los Jueves De Ana Postigo**) on Thursday.
- El Yeite Tango Club (**elyeite.com.ar** and Facebook **El Yeite Tango Club**), Monday and Thursday in Palermo.
- De Querusa (Facebook **De Querusa**) in Boedo on Thursday.
- Práctica X (**practicax.net** and Facebook **Practica X**) is back from an extended vacation and is on Tuesday night in Palermo.
- The Club Independencia events on various nights in San Telmo; try Milonga en Orsay (Facebook **Milonga en Orsay**) on Thursday.
- Centro Cultural Torquato Tasso in San Telmo; try the Sunday night La Milonga del Tasso (Facebook **La Milonga del Tasso**).

Finding the Tango Venues

To get an idea of where the tango venues of Buenos Aires are located, download a PDF copy of the Caserón Porteño Tango Map, North and South sections (see **The Listings** for details), and print it before you come — even if it's an old version, it will give you the idea. It shows the locations of around fifty Buenos Aires tango venues. The district names marked on the map are some of the *barrios porteños* (the forty-eight official districts of Buenos Aires much referred to in the lyrics of tangos): some examples are San Nicolás, Balvanera, Recoleta, Palermo, Monserrat and San Telmo. *Porteños* (the people of Buenos Aires) also use lots of other convenient, but unofficial, district names for cultural or commercial areas within the city: some examples of these are Centro, Microcentro, Barrio Norte, Congreso and Once. In fact, these days it's more common to hear the unofficial names than the official ones, and that's why I point them out, though they are not marked on all maps.

One glance at the red dots indicating the venues on the Caserón Porteño Map will tell you that Buenos Aires tango is spread far and wide throughout the city. Despite this, there are clusters of tango venues in the following three parts of Buenos Aires, and you may want to take this into account when deciding where to stay (and for a bit more advice on that and the barrios themselves, see **Sleep** in **Part 4**):

The Centro: includes parts of the official San Nicolás, Monserrat, Balvanera and Recoleta barrios. The Centro is not an official barrio, but it is a convenient label for the most central part of the city; the most downtown sub-section of the Centro is known as the Microcentro. Confitería Ideal, El Beso, Porteño y Bailarín, Casa de Galicia, Nuevo Salón La Argentina, Aires Tangueros and La Nacional are located in or very close to the Centro.

Palermo: lies to the north of the Centro. Salón Canning, Club Villa Malcolm, La Viruta, El Yeite, Práctica X, Sala Siranush and Club Fulgor are located in or very close to Palermo.

San Telmo: lies to the south of the Centro. Buenos Ayres Club, Plaza Dorrego, Cochabamba 444, Centro Cultural Torquato Tasso and Club Independencia are in San Telmo. In addition, Centro Región Leonesa and Lo de Celia Tango Club are located in the adjacent barrio of Constitución.

The remaining venues I've mentioned are further afield, and to visit them all you'll need to travel to the northern barrios of Belgrano, Colegiales, Villa Urquiza and Saavedra, and to the western barrios of San Cristóbal, Once, Abasto, Almagro, Boedo and Flores.

The Week at a Glance

The first thing I did, as I began to know of a few different milongas in Buenos Aires, was draw a grid in my notebook: days across the top, milongas underneath. Thus I planned my dancing week. You already know of at least thirty weekly milongas and prácticas in Buenos Aires. And now, here is a selection of them, slotted into a handy planner — perhaps your first week of dance possibilities, at a glance.

	Monday	Tuesday	Wednesday
Tourist-circuit Famous venues, accustomed to tourists; mixed age range. Stick to **Sallycat's Rules for Happy Tango in Buenos Aires** for best results.	Parakultural in Salón Canning from 11pm	Porteño y Bailarín from 10.30pm Parakultural in Salón Canning from 11pm	Try Sueño Porteño or La Milonguita (Traditional but relaxed) or Maldita Milonga (Informal with a live orchestra) – see below
Traditional Authentic milongas that can be more conservative and formal in style; older age range. Adhere to the códigos to fit in and gain the respect of the regulars.	El Arranque in Nuevo Salón La Argentina from 3pm (also Tuesday, Thursday and Saturday) El Maipú in La Nacional from 6pm Lunes de Tango in Club Gricel from 9pm	Nuevo Chique in Casa de Galicia from 4pm Cachirulo in El Beso from 8pm Derecho Viejo in Plaza Bohemia from 6.30pm	A Puro Tango in Salón Canning from 4pm Sueño Porteño in Boedo Tango from 7pm La Milonguita in Sala Siranush from 7pm La Piccola Milonga in Aires Tangueros from 10pm
Informal Relaxed milongas and prácticas, especially popular with the younger generation. Do one of the classes beforehand, and make friends to dance with later on.	El Motivo in Club Villa Malcolm from 10pm Bendita Milonga in Buenos Ayres Club from 10.30pm El Yeite from 11.30pm (also Thursday)	Milonga10 in Club Fulgor from 11pm Tango Queer in Buenos Ayres Club from 10pm La Catedral Club from 11pm (open every night; see website)	La Maria práctica in La Catedral from 3pm Maldita Milonga in Buenos Ayres Club from 10.30pm Fruto Dulce in Villa Malcolm from 10.30pm

(handwritten annotations, top of page) радость он о своем игри е Олеи · 8 ир ne — Вторник — Color Tango Salo сои ниje резерваи

Thursday	Friday	Saturday	Sunday
Niño Bien in Centro Región Leonesa from 10.30pm *(handwritten: de Los zueea)*	El Abrazo Tango Club in Confitería Ideal from 2pm Parakultural in Salón Canning from 11pm Unitango Club in Confitería Ideal from 11pm	Club Sunderland from 10.30pm — not great for solo dancers; go in a couple or with friends	La Milonga de Paula y Carlos in Confitería Ideal from 3pm *(handwritten: English)* Milonga Placita del Pañuelo Blanco in Plaza Dorrego from 8pm Porteño y Bailarín from 10.30pm
El Nuevo Chiqué in Casa de Galicia from 4pm Lujos in El Beso from 6.30pm La Cachila in Club Gricel from 8pm	El Maipú in Casa de Galicia from 6pm La Milonga de Elsita in Plaza Bohemia from 6pm La Baldosa in Salón El Pial from 11pm — not great for solo dancers; go in a couple or with friends	Milonga de Los Consagrados in Centro Región Leonesa from 4.30pm J.L. in La Nacional from 8pm Cachirulo in Club Villa Malcolm from 9pm Milonga de las Morochas in El Beso from 10.30pm	Lo de Celia Tango Club from 6pm Lujos in Plaza Bohemia from 6.30pm La Milonguita in Centro Montañés from 8pm Domingos de El Beso from 10pm
Jueves en Cochabamba 444 from 10.30pm Soho Tango in Club Villa Malcolm from 10.30pm La Viruta from half past midnight (also on Wednesday from 11.30pm)	Tangocool in Club Villa Malcolm from 11.30pm La Marshàll in El Beso from 11.30pm La Viruta from midnight	La Glorieta, outdoors, from 7pm Milonga10 in Club Fulgor from 11pm La Viruta from midnight	La Glorieta, outdoors, from 7pm La Milonga del Tasso in Centro Cultural Torquato Tasso from 10pm La Viruta from half past midnight

(handwritten, bottom of page: come at 3am · at 4am — media lunas Rosalina · come at 3am)

Part 4

BUENOS AIRES PRACTICALITIES FOR TANGO DANCERS

The Big Decision Tango tour or go it alone?

If you're weighing up whether to travel independently and discover tango in Buenos Aires for yourself, or whether to join an organised group tour and let someone else make the decisions for you, then this section is for you.

If you come here with a group, you won't have to worry about the travel and accommodation arrangements. Your schedule of classes might be prearranged, and the milongas you'll visit decided in advance. You'll even have a ready-made group of English-speaking friends to hang out with. If you don't speak Spanish, or need assistance, then help will be on tap too. All of this 'being looked after' can be very reassuring.

On the other hand, if you make the trip alone, you might feel a bit apprehensive at first: you won't have anyone to hold your hand. But tango-wise, there could be some advantages. For a start, you'll be in full control of where you dance your tango. A group tour might only take you to the milongas that can accommodate groups of tourists, or to the favourites of the tour organiser, but what if your 'tango homes' lie elsewhere? Secondly, if you are a solo dancer who wants to access the best possible dances, you will want to be seen as committed: you'll want to enter the milongas alone or perhaps with a friend, and not as one of a big bunch of tourists. Thirdly, I am convinced that to really get under the skin of the tango culture here, you need to fit in rather than stand out. I know I've said that to be seen is all-important, but only if it's for the right reasons: great dancing, elegance, magnetism, behaviour that shows you are in the know. You want to create a ripple of intriguing beauty in the milonga (*I'm slipping into this seat next to you as if I've been doing it all my life*), not a tsunami (*We're taking over this whole corner of the room as noisily as we possibly can*). In my experience, it's easier to connect with the locals and regulars when you are alone.

There could be some tango upsides to a group tour. You'll have those ready-made 'friends': someone to dance with, someone to show you off at the start of a milonga or someone to partner in classes. Your teachers might accompany you to the milongas and dance with you, or introduce you to some of their friends who might dance with you too. The level of energy at your milonga table could be high, and so could attract attention, but I'm afraid the question has to be, whose?

For my own Buenos Aires tango adventure — because I was, at that point in time, quite needful of someone to assist me with my travel arrangements — I chose a mix of part independent and part organised, in the form of a packaged travel experience bought on the internet, which included a tango teacher for a month (who turned out to be Ariel), some basic hostel accommodation (where I met my first tanguera partner-in-crime), and four weeks of Spanish classes (enough to get me started). Dancing-wise, I did it alone in the milongas. Yes, perhaps I learned some things the hard way. But if I hadn't, I wouldn't have been inspired to write this book. My advice, when making any choice at all, is to go with your instinct, your gut instinct, and ultimately, your heart. What do you really feel is right for you: independent travel or tango tour? Go for the thing you truly want, and I think the rest will take care of itself. After all, perhaps you can try the other option next time around.

Sleep Where to stay

Choosing a location

Which area of the city should you stay in?

Most tango tourists want to be close to the tango venues. The challenge is, as I explained in **Finding the Tango Venues** in **Part 3**, that the tango is spread all over the city. However, there are three distinct clusters: in the Centro, in Palermo (to the north of the Centro) and in San Telmo (to the south of the Centro). So, to be roughly in the centre of everything tango-wise, you could stay in the Centro. But it can be far too full-on-city-centre for some. Indeed many tango tourists opt either for trendy Palermo or for bohemian San Telmo, as good alternatives. Let me show you around all three areas, to help you choose.

The Centro (mutated slightly, to give you the best options)

Where's the most central part of the city, suitable for tango tourists? You can find it easily. On the Caserón Porteño Tango Map South (see **The Listings** in **Part 3** for where to get your hands on it online) or on any map of Buenos Aires, mark the four major avenidas, Rivadavia, Pueyrredón, 9 de Julio and Las Heras, and find an address in the resulting box, or not too far from it. A home in this part of the city will place you closest to the cluster of tango venues in the Centro, and roughly equidistant from the San Telmo and Palermo clusters. You'll still be far from some venues, but that can't be avoided, wherever you stay. This central area varies in character: the closer you are to Rivadavia, the more hectic and less refined; and the nearer to Las Heras, in the areas called Recoleta and Barrio Norte, the plusher and smarter your surroundings will be.

The Centro actually extends across Avenida 9 de Julio into the downtown area known as the Microcentro. The Microcentro is home to government offices, the city's financial district, many tourist sights, the pedestrianised Florida and Lavalle streets, and a great deal of beautiful architecture. I would personally prefer to visit this part of the city as a sightseer than to stay in it. It's just too noisy and manic for me, and too touristy. Walking the length of Florida can feel overwhelming when it's teeming with people. This area draws tourists, so the restaurants and cafés can be overpriced, and because the district is more commercial than residential, it can be difficult to find a supermarket or greengrocer if you want to cook for yourself.

As explained in **Finding the Tango Venues** in **Part 3**, some of the official barrio names used for the most central parts of the city are San Nicolás, Monserrat, Balvanera and Recoleta. Unofficial names are Centro (which includes parts of all these four), Microcentro (the most downtown part of the Centro), Barrio Norte (the part of Recoleta around Avenida Santa Fe), Congreso (parts of Balvanera, San Nicolás and Monserrat around the Congreso building) and Once (a commercial district spanning a part of Balvanera). Districts can cover wide areas though. Check each accommodation address on the map to see how central it is and how close to a main avenida (good for taxis, shops and banks) and to the *Subte* (the official name for the subway); the area around Once mainline train station is probably best avoided as it's known to be less safe than other central areas.

The Centro is bustling and more mass-market commercial than boutique. On the upside, there's plenty of everything you need, like shops, banks, traditional cafés and restaurants, theatres, cinemas and public transport; on the downside, it can feel claustrophobic and exhausting, especially on and around Avenida Corrientes.

If you don't mind scruffier and slightly edgier, you could extend your search of the central part of the city, from Avenida Rivadavia towards Avenida Belgrano, further into the district called Monserrat, where there is plenty of beautiful old architecture and some of the most authentic restaurants and cafés in Buenos Aires. This section of the city could suit the more confident or well-travelled types, or people who know the city already: it's well located for the most popular Traditional-style tango venues, is close to San Telmo and is loved by many tango travellers, but I think that first-timers of fainter heart might prefer the slightly more upmarket vibe that prevails in the streets closer to Avenida Santa Fe than to Avenida Belgrano.

Palermo

There is a cluster of tango venues in Palermo, and the majority fit into my Informal category, so if my description of the **Informal Venues/ Milongas/Prácticas** in **Part 3** sounds like your style, then a Palermo address could suit you. It would also put you on the side of the city closest to Salón Canning, which is in Palermo, La Glorieta in Belgrano, and Club Sunderland in Villa Urquiza. Palermo is on the opposite side of the city centre to San Telmo. From Palermo Subte station to the downtown city centre (the 9 de Julio Subte station, which is more or less underneath the famous Obelisco) on the Line D takes about fifteen minutes, when the trains are running smoothly.

Palermo is huge and varied in character, with different parts referred to by different names: Palermo Soho, Palermo Viejo, Palermo Hollywood (the part furthest from the city centre), Palermo Queens (the part that overlaps with Villa Crespo) and Palermo Chico (the part nearest to the river). Palermo is known for having a hip and trendy vibe, with designer boutiques and upmarket restaurants far more common than large supermarkets or traditional-style cafés. It's also closest to the majority of the city centre's most popular green and open spaces: the Rosedal in Parque 3 de Febrero, the Jardín Botanico (Botanical Garden), the Jardín Japonés (Japanese Garden), the Campo Argentino de Polo (where the city's big polo matches are played) and the Hipódromo Argentino racecourse. When considering an address billed as being in Palermo, be careful to ask how far you will be from a main avenida and a Subte station (for fast access to the city centre). It's generally thought of as pretty safe, but there are plenty of quiet back streets between the main avenidas and the noisier streets (packed with restaurants, clubs and bars), and I wouldn't wander in the darker spots at night on my own. When assessing whether an address is well-located in Palermo, stick to the east side of Avenida Cordóba, avoid the mainline railway that separates Palermo Soho and Palermo Hollywood, and then for convenience, perhaps try to be within a few blocks of Avenida Santa Fe and the Subte Line D.

Heading further away from the Centro, on the edge of Palermo towards Belgrano, is the small barrio called Las Cañitas. Villagey in feel, with plenty of trendy bars and restaurants, it's the closest residential district to the polo ground, and very pleasant. Its nearest Subte station is Ministro Carranza on the Line D, perhaps a ten-minute walk away. Beyond Palermo is Belgrano, a popular residential district, of good character. Belgrano is home to La Glorieta (see **7 Informal Places to Try First** in **Part 3**), and Barrio Chino, the small Chinatown of Buenos Aires.

San Telmo

There is a cluster of tango venues in San Telmo and they fall into my Informal category, as for Palermo. For more Traditional-style tango, San Telmo puts you on the side of the city closest to Centro Región Leonesa and Lo de Celia in the barrio of Constitución, and to Casa de Galicia and La Nacional in Monserrat. You'd be on the opposite side of the city to the venues in Palermo and beyond. For good information on San Telmo and its tango venues, including some that I haven't mentioned in this book, take a look at the **welcomesantelmo.com** website.

San Telmo, with its touristy tango-dinner shows, antique markets and colonial buildings, either being gentrified or being left to fall to bits, feels like a world of its own: a little town within a city. Pretty and bohemian when you're soaking up the sun at a café in Plaza Dorrego in summer; shabby, shuttered up and not always that safe when night falls. To get to the city centre, you can take the slightly scruffy Subte Line C that runs along the edge of the barrio (takes about 10 minutes from the station San Juan), or you can walk (about 20 minutes), though it's best to avoid the bus routes for your walk because the streets are narrow and it can get noisy. Large supermarkets and banks are not plentiful in the back streets of San Telmo and you might have to walk to Avenida 9 de Julio to find an ATM (there are a couple of banks with LINK-network cash-machines near its corner with Carlos Calvo). The atmospheric indoor El Mercado de San Telmo (bordered by Defensa, Bolivar, Carlos Calvo and Estados Unidos, and with entrances off all four of those streets) has fresh vegetables, fruit, cheese, eggs, meat and bread, and there's a smallish Dia supermarket on Bolivar street opposite the market exit. On Sundays, San Telmo gets taken over by the street market of crafts, antiques and souvenirs and the accompanying hordes of tourists: if you feel the need to escape the crowds, Parque Lezama, on the far edge of the barrio, is a lovely green space for a walk, and is home to the interesting Museo Histórico Nacional (National History Museum) in the mansion situated in the park, at the end of Avenida Caseros.

Further away from the city centre, beyond San Telmo, is the barrio of La Boca, which you will almost certainly visit (for a great view of La Boca, see my sightseeing suggestions under **See**), though it isn't somewhere you'd want to stay. To the east of San Telmo, bordering the river, begins the Puerto Madero area: it's full of high-rise luxury apartments, renovated dockland warehouses, expensive restaurants and some five-star hotels, but feels cut off from the rest of the city, in part because of some major and extremely busy heavy-traffic routes, which must be crossed to get there. On the far side of Puerto Madero is the Parque Natural y Reserva Ecológica Costanera Sur (**porlareserva.org.ar**), a stunning wetlands nature reserve that can be explored either on foot or by rented bicycle (try La Bicicleta Naranja at **labicicletanaranja.com.ar** or Urban Biking at **en.urbanbiking.com**).

Choosing your accommodation

When it comes to accommodation, the most popular options for tango tourists are:

- A room in a shared apartment
- A hostel
- A bed and breakfast (B&B)
- A tango guest house
- A rented apartment
- A hotel

Here are a few things to think about before you decide on which of them might be right for you.

What is your accommodation budget per day in US dollars?

Most tourist accommodation is quoted in US dollars. You might have to pay in cash — if credit cards aren't accepted, check carefully how much you will need to hand over on arrival, so that you can bring it with you.

What season will it be?

Spring (September to November) and autumn (March to May) are delightful months in Buenos Aires and the season need not impact your choice of accommodation. In summer (December to February) good ventilation needs to be a priority — fans and/or air conditioning, balconies or inner courtyards are desirable; with windows open all day and possibly night (if you can cope with the mosquitoes), good security and a quiet street are also more important. In winter (June to August) reliable heating is a must. In both high summer and midwinter you might also want to be closer to key public transport links and available taxis.

How long are you intending to stay?

Hotels and hostels offer rates that vary by the tourist season. Bed and breakfasts and tango guest houses sometimes give discounts to those staying more than a few weeks. Shared apartments usually want longer term tenants and are not over-keen on a stay of less than one month. If you are coming for months rather than weeks, you should consider booking comfortable accommodation for your arrival, to give you time to settle in to the city and check out longer term possibilities in person. Having tried it myself, I would be very wary of committing to more than a few weeks either in lodgings or a district that you haven't seen. In my case (with a plan to be here for between three and twelve months), I stayed in a single room in a hostel for a month, and I used that time to get to know the city's districts and to search for an apartment. I was lucky because the hostel was in a decent part of Palermo, but I am still very glad I didn't book it for longer because the room was tiny, the hostel was too noisy for me and I couldn't wait to leave the communal bathrooms behind!

Do you want to share?

If you are coming in a group, you may be able to negotiate a group booking (with appropriate discount) or take a flat together. But if you are coming on your own, you need to think about whether you want to share, and what: bedroom, bathroom, kitchen, living areas? Also consider what kind of people you want to share with: noisy young party-goers, other tango dancers, sophisticated travellers? You can get some idea of who stays where by reading the online reviews on the websites I mention on the next few pages.

How much service do you want?

Hosts can look after the property (decoration, repairs, security, cleaning, fresh linen, etc), and they can also look after you (arrange airport transfers, speak your language, know about tango, explain their city, be around on a regular basis when your new questions come up, help you if you are ill or have a crisis). Most places do the first, while some bed and breakfasts and tango guest houses also do the second. Some rented apartments provide little service, with managers difficult to contact when the toilet is blocked or the hot water won't work. Ask questions about what kind of support you will get after you have handed over your money, and, if possible, read reviews (or talk to other guests) before booking.

What are your must-haves and can't-stands?

Check (by email) that your must-haves and can't-stands will/will not be present before you commit to a booking: print and bring any written confirmations with you. Common must-haves are: free WiFi or cable internet, easy late-night entry to the building, access to a landline telephone (though you will have to use a calling card to call abroad or to local mobile phones), smoking/non-smoking as preferred, fans or air conditioning in the summer, access to a balcony or terrace. Can't-stands should address any allergies (pets, smoking, synthetic bedding), and might include: noisy bus routes outside the bedroom windows (common in Buenos Aires), loud nightclubs or bars nearby, or insufficient heating in the winter.

The accommodation options and where to find them

Hotels can work out on the expensive side in Buenos Aires, so many tango tourists opt for one of the several alternatives. Here's a bit more information about each, so you can get an idea of whether any of them might suit you.

A room in a shared house or apartment with all rooms rented out individually by the manager, generally on a longer term basis; shared kitchen and bathroom facilities.

Best for	Longer stays (probably more than a month); independent, flexible and tolerant people.
Not for	The obsessively tidy, or very light sleepers.
Warning	Don't be pressured into paying a big deposit before you get here. Best to have a good look around first.
Ask for	Photos of bathroom(s) and kitchen and check how many bathrooms there are — more than three rooms to a bathroom can be a problem.
Price range	From shoestring to moderate.
Search in	Start with Craigslist (**buenosaires.en.craigslist.org** in rooms/shared, under housing) or **airbnb.com**

A hostel, of the calmer variety (some can be party, party, party... but you can get an idea of the vibe from the websites of individual places — good ones will have detailed descriptions, lots of photographs and a map of the location), usually offering both bunk rooms (dorms) and some private rooms.

Best for	Shorter stays (a couple of weeks); independent, flexible and tolerant people; people who want to make friends — especially if the hostel has a tango theme, it could be a good place to meet other tango dancers.
Not for	The obsessively tidy or private, or very light sleepers.
Warning	Check there is adequate security for your things — most places provide cupboards or metal cages you can lock with your own padlock, but in some hostels there are insufficient lockers for the number of people. Make sure the standard of cleanliness meets your requirements.

Ask for	Photos of bathroom(s) and kitchen. Hours of access. Restrictions on noise levels in the hostel (which could dictate how many hours of sleep you're likely to get!).
Price range	From shoestring to moderate. Private rooms are comparatively expensive — if you want one, it might be worth considering a bed and breakfast.
Search in	**hostelworld.com** or **hostelbuenosaires.com** or **tripadvisor.com**

A room at a bed and breakfast, with shared or private bathroom: there are usually up to about eight rooms in total, with (generally) 'tourist' standards for bathrooms and linen, and hosts who speak some English.

Best for	Shorter to medium stays (up to a month). People who prefer a balance of privacy and care from their hosts; first-timers in Buenos Aires.
Not for	The obsessively private (common areas are shared), or those who like to cook banquets (kitchens are for simple meal preparation only, and some places don't even allow that).
Warning	The best places have a good, informative website — it should tell you about the services offered and the barrio, and have a map and lots of photos. Try to find independent online reviews (not just put on the website by the owner).
Ask for	Photos of the bathroom, and number of people you will share it with. Frequency of maid service. Hours of access.
Price range	From moderate (shared bathroom) to expensive (private bathroom). Ask for discounts for longer stays.
Search in	**bedandbreakfast.com** or **bbonline.com** or **airbnb.com** or **tripadvisor.com**

A room at a tango guest house: this is a special type of bed and breakfast that caters for guests (and groups) who come especially to dance tango; usually offers a space for practising your tango, organises classes and may be linked to particular tango schools or teachers.

Best for	Shorter stays (a couple of weeks); first-timers in Buenos Aires; people keen to befriend other tango dancers.
Not for	The very independent or those who intend to sample a range of dance teachers.
Warning	These places may have ties to particular dance teachers/schools, with free lessons included — an advantage if that works for you, but a waste if you don't use them. Could be noisy at night, with tango dancers coming and going at all hours! Otherwise, same warnings as for B&Bs.
Ask for	Details of included extras, such as free tango classes. Otherwise, same as for B&Bs.
Price range	Wide, depending on level of luxury, and whether tango classes are included. At the top end, a private bathroom may lift the price to expensive. May have a discount for groups.
Search in	**bedandbreakfast.com** or **bbonline.com** or **tripadvisor.com**

An apartment that can usually be rented by the week or month: non-resident foreigners generally rent through an agency with prices in US dollars; there is a completely different system for locals — rent in Argentine pesos, long contract periods, and the need for a guarantor.

Best for	Longer stays (a month or more); independent people.
Not for	People who need a lot of looking after.
Warning	Use a reputable company. If possible, best to have a look around before paying: try the hot water, toilet flush, stove, lights, air conditioning and/or fans or heating, internet connection, all keys; check for spare linen.

Ask for	Photos of bathroom(s) and kitchen. Details of air conditioning, fans or heating, depending on the season. Check which floor the apartment is on, whether it is located on a bus route, and whether it's at the front or back of the building — bus routes can be extremely noisy and the buses run all night; higher floors and apartments located at the back of buildings tend to be quieter. Frequency of maid service. Possibly an email address for a previous foreign tenant, so you can solicit your own reference, or check online reviews.
Price range	From moderate to expensive (but cheaper if you can share the cost with friends). Weekly rates can be significantly higher than the monthly rates.
Search in	**bytargentina.com** or **bahomerental.com** among many other local rental companies, or try **airbnb.com** where every kind of accommodation is offered by individual owners, including apartments.

Come and go How to get around

There is no escaping it. If you want to dance tango in Buenos Aires you will have to travel at all hours. My **20 Places to Try First** are spread citywide, and when you start to explore beyond those you could be travelling even further afield. So, what are your options for getting from your accommodation to your first tango class of the day, to the matinée milonga of your choice, to the venue where you'll dance the night away, and finally back to your bed at the end of the tango marathon?

Radio taxis

If you are here on holiday and not on a drastic budget, you'll like the taxis: they are numerous and convenient, though less economical than they used to be, as prices have risen quite steeply in the last few years. They are the safest option for getting home from the milongas, in the early hours of the morning.

Taxis in Buenos Aires are painted black and yellow. The drivers are called *taxistas* or *choferes*. If you are concerned about safety, take radio taxis: they usually have writing on *all four doors* and a radio taxi light on the roof. Radio taxis should be safest because they are normally connected with and responsible to a hub: my taxi broke down on the way to Ezeiza International Airport, but because it was a radio taxi, the driver was able to contact the hub and get another cab sent out fast. Non-radio taxis, which might have writing on the front doors only, and no light on the roof, are operated by individuals: the majority are completely above board and honest; however, a few are not. Available taxis show a red LIBRE light in the front window. Flag taxis down in the street, preferably in the direction you wish to travel to avoid costly detours. Once in the taxi:

- Give the address by street intersection (two street names) rather than a single street name and a number. Say the street of the actual address first. For example, for Salón Canning, say *Scalabrini Ortiz y Cabrera*. Then you can follow with the actual address, if you wish to be dropped outside the door, *Scalabrini Ortiz mil trescientos treinta y uno* (1331). Taxi drivers don't usually know the names of tango venues or milongas, so you'll have to know and give the address, as I've described.

• Make sure the driver puts the *reloj* (meter) on: he will usually do it just after you move off.

• You don't need to tip the driver.

• Use small denomination notes, as close as possible to the total: be careful if paying with a $100 peso note, as an occasional scam is for the note to be swapped for a forgery, which is then refused and handed back to you — the driver gets the real note, you get the forgery and the driver insists that you pay him all over again.

• To solve any problem involving a lack of *monedas* (coins; see **Spend** for more details), you or the driver may round things to the nearest peso to help each other out.

• Pay up fast when the journey ends. Have your money ready because when the taxi stops, the meter doesn't (until you've handed over the fare), and if you take five minutes fumbling around for the money, you'll end up paying more.

• The more knowledgeable you can appear about the route, the better placed you are to avoid the taxi driver taking you on deliberate detours to earn a few extra pesos: get in a taxi that's going in the direction you wish to travel; ask for the destination by an intersection of streets, not by a street and a number; and if your Castellano and street knowledge are up to it, suggest the route you know to be the shortest or quickest.

Subte

The *Subte* (the official name of the metro/subway/underground train; see **www.subte.com.ar**) is easy, safe to use and very reasonably priced. Buy tickets at the *boletería* (ticket booth) in the Subte station and to save queuing, buy tickets with ten journeys on them — say *diez* (ten). Entrances to the subway stations are clearly marked with the letter-name (A, B, C, D, E and H) of the line, the colour (look for big Smartie-like circles overhead) allocated to the line, and the direction of travel (indicated by the name of the end-of-line station) to be accessed via that particular entrance. At some stations you can't get to both platforms once you are underground, so you must enter via the correct entrance for the direction you want. The subway starts around 6am but stops running fairly early, about 10.30–11pm, so you might be able to use it to get to a night milonga, but unless you stop for breakfast somewhere first, you won't be able to use it to get back home afterwards.

Colectivos

Most tango dancers who stay in Buenos Aires for any length of time come to love the *colectivos* (buses): they are cheap; they enable criss-crossing of the city on routes that the Subte cannot reach; most run all night (so you can use them to get both to and from the milongas), though with a reduced service; and you can get fabulous views as you travel. But it does take a bit of time and work to understand which bus you want to catch and how to pay. If you decide you want to take advantage of the bus system, use the website **mapa.buenosaires.gob.ar** and click '¿*Cómo Llego*?' to input your *Desde* (From) and *Hasta* (To) locations to find out which bus will work for you. Alternatively, get your hands on a pocket-sized *GUIA "T" de Bolsillo* (Pocket GUIDE "T"), sold on the Subte by travelling vendors or at street newsstands. This little guide details the bus routes, though it can seem a little baffling at first.

For travelling by bus in Buenos Aires:

• Locate the bus stop: find the number of your bus marked some-where on the bus shelter, bus-stop pole or wall nearby. When you see your bus approaching, stick out your arm to indicate that you want to get on, otherwise it may not stop.

• Once on the bus, you must tell the bus driver either the ticket price you want or the street to which you are travelling (the street that crosses the main route); he will then set the coin-operated ticket machine (normally located behind the driver) to issue you with the appropriately priced ticket. Insert your coins into the slot, usually at the top of the ticket machine. The machines do give change. Take your ticket and hang on to it for the journey; it's possible that a ticket inspector may appear.

- Press the buzzer (located on the metal poles near the doors, or sometimes above the doors) before the bus stop you want. If nobody presses, the bus may not stop.
- Get on and off quickly, as the bus driver will want to shut the doors and get moving. Get off using the centre or back doors only.
- Be aware that the majority of streets in Buenos Aires are one-way, therefore buses take different routes going and coming back.
- The seats at the front must be vacated if someone more deserving of a seat gets on the bus: the elderly, the pregnant, parents with children, etc. You will notice that Argentines are very quick to give up their seat in these cases. Do the same to avoid complaints or hard stares from fellow passengers.

A card-payment system has now been introduced for bus travel and it offers an alternative (and in late 2012, it was a cheaper alternative) to buying your tickets with coins. You'll need a SUBE card (**www.sube.gob.ar** and click *Centros de Obtención* for where to obtain one) — you will probably need to show your passport and fill in a form, and there is a small fee. You can buy credit for the SUBE card anywhere you see the SUBE sign (see *Centros de Carga* on the SUBE website). If you use a card to pay for your bus journey, tell the driver the price of your journey or where you are going. He will set the amount on the card paypoint (located either to your right as you board the bus or behind the driver, next to the coin-operated machine), and you hold your card up to the base of the machine for the payment to be deducted from your card. If you pay with a card, you don't get a ticket; having the card is your proof of purchase, it seems.

Holders of Monedero (**www.monedero.com.ar**) cards need to know that, because of a change in systems, from December 2012 you will not be able to pay for bus or subway travel with either a Monedero card or the new Monedero 'tag' which will replace it.

Walk!

Buenos Aires is easy to navigate, and if you have the time to walk a few blocks between tango classes you will give yourself the chance to truly feel the city's heartbeat. When you walk, look up, because so much beauty in Buenos Aires is above the ground floor; do not miss the towers especially. But look down too. There are huge numbers of dogs in the city, and many owners don't clean up after them. Plus, there are many potholes and wobbly slabs in the pavements, which can squirt filthy water up your leg, after rain.

Be sensible about walking at night. Stick to the main avenidas (where there is usually life after dark); avoid deserted back streets; walk just as far as you need to get a taxi after the milonga and wait with a friend if you can — all common sense.

The streets of Buenos Aires are arranged on a grid. The streets are either *avenidas* (the main avenues such as Las Heras, Santa Fe, Córdoba, Corrientes, Rivadavia, Avenida de Mayo, Paseo Colón, 9 de Julio, Callao, Pueyrredón and Scalabrini Ortiz) or *calles* (the streets running parallel to the main avenidas). Many avenidas and calles change their names as they cross the city, for example, as they cross Avenida Rivadavia (Callao becomes Entre Ríos, Puerreydón becomes Jujuy, etc.). With few exceptions, every street or avenue is divided into *cuadras* (blocks) of one hundred numbers. Easy.

Getting from and to the airport

When you arrive at Ezeiza International Airport, you can safely organise a taxi, on the spot, from one of the pre-pay booths either inside or outside the terminal building. I've used Taxi Ezeiza, with its distinctive white cars (**taxiezeiza.com.ar**). There's a set price to the city centre. You pay at the desk inside the terminal and they give you a voucher to hand to the driver. Taxi Ezeiza offers a facility to book both arrival and departure taxis, in advance, online. The website includes current prices. Manuel Tienda León (**www.tiendaleon.com.ar**) offers a bus service with fixed drop-off points. Silver Star Transport (**silverstarcar.com**) is a luxury English-spoken option, bookable only in advance.

Spend All things money

I remember the first time I went to Comme il Faut to buy tango shoes, in March 2007. I asked for the price. The reply was *Three hundred* (ah, those were the days, when top-of-the-range tango shoes cost so little...). I paid with a credit card because I was too embarrassed to ask if it was US dollars or Argentine pesos. It was pesos, thank God, but I often laugh at myself, that coming from England where my first-ever (rather plain) tango shoes had seemed very expensive, I would have actually been prepared to pay three hundred US dollars for those sexier-than-I'd-ever-imagined shoes! You can pay by credit card in Comme il Faut, but in Buenos Aires, credit cards are not always accepted. You're going to need cash in hand. Here's the lowdown on all things money.

The currency

It's the Argentine peso and its symbol is $. Don't confuse it with the symbol for dollars in the United States, which in Argentina takes the form U$D or USD or US$, since payment for some things might be in dollars or pesos. For example, $10 is most likely to mean ten pesos *not* ten US dollars. Some shops accept US dollars and they will do the conversion at the day's exchange rate (or most likely at better than the day's rate, as US dollars are a highly desired commodity). Some prices might be quoted in US dollars for tourists: accommodation prices, flight tickets, tours, some private tango lessons with the more famous names... don't be as shy as I was — if in doubt, ask: *Dólares o pesos?*

Getting your hands on your money

The easiest option for obtaining pesos in Buenos Aires, is the *Cajero Automático* or ATM. There are ATMs inside most banks, usually with instructions in English, linked to either the BANELCO (red) or LINK (green) networks. To enter the bank outside banking hours (10am to 3pm, Monday to Friday), you have to swipe your card in the door. If there is only one ATM, Argentines queue in the street to give each other privacy, and enter one at a time. Put all your money and cards away before leaving the bank.

Bank branches with ATMs tend to be on the main avenidas of the city. To find out if there is an ATM near you, check the websites of BANELCO (**https://w3.banelco.com.ar** and use the *BUSCADOR DE CAJEROS* to search under Capital Federal and your barrio), and LINK (*BUSCADOR DE CAJEROS* at **www.redlink.com.ar**).

ATMs often run out of money, break down or are closed for service. Occasionally, finding a functioning ATM can take a while (especially between 3pm and 5pm when they get restocked). Beware that in some banks the Cajero Automáticos stand alongside other machines that look like ATMs, but are only for use by customers of the bank; make sure the one you use is clearly marked Cajero Automático with either a BANELCO or LINK sign, and not with *Solo para clientes del banco* (Only for clients of the bank).

ATMs, by default, dispense $100 peso notes: if you request $500 pesos you will usually receive five $100 peso notes, which can be unwelcome for low-value purchases and taxi fares. To obtain smaller denominations, select the 'Other Amount' option and enter $490 pesos. Then the ATM will be forced to give you smaller notes, assuming it has them. There is normally a limit on the amount of pesos you can withdraw per transaction and per day. People report many different experiences.

If you bring U$D traveller's cheques, these can be changed in some banks and exchange bureaus, but you might have to stand in a long queue. Changing cash can be faster. To change traveller's cheques or cash, you'll need to show your passport. A reputable exchange bureau is Banco Piano (**www.bancopiano.com.ar**), with several branches throughout the city. In Ezeiza International Airport there is only one option for changing cash into pesos, Banco Nación, though there is also an ATM in the arrivals hall. Once you are in the city centre you may see and hear of *casas de cambio* (exchange houses) offering a better rate than the banks for cash dollars; if you decide to go for it, do be on your guard for scams or for forged notes, won't you? It might well all work out fine and in your favour, but then again you should keep your eyes peeled, because, in all such unofficial matters, there is no recourse if things don't go to plan.

Credit cards are increasingly accepted, but not everywhere: check first to avoid difficulties. You will usually be asked for ID, and often only a passport will suffice. Sometimes I've been able to use my photo UK Driving Licence or a photocopy of my passport ID page, but not always. When completing the credit card receipt, you have to sign and give your ID document number. Before travelling, check with your bank that your cards will work in Argentina.

It's a good idea to bring some U$D cash as a reserve and to pay for any large U$D cash expenses that you know about in advance, such as your accommodation and private tango lessons with famous names. Holders of USA bank accounts tell me that Xoom (**xoom.com**) offers a reliable and cost-effective way to transfer and convert U$D into pesos; I haven't yet been able to find anything similar for those of us without a USA bank account.

Monedas

There can often be a shortage of *monedas* (coins of $2 and $1 peso, and 50, 25, 10 and 5 centavos) in Buenos Aires. This may affect you if you decide to travel on the buses and are paying with cash rather than a SUBE card, or if you have a laundry machine in your building that takes coins. In case you find the lack of monedas a little stressful, here are three ways you can get your hands on them:

• Go to a bank for between $5 pesos and (if you are very fortunate, and the coins are available) $20 pesos in change. You may have to stand in line for quite a while. When you get to the cashier, simply say, *Monedas, por favor*. Hand over your $20 peso note and see what you get back.
• Eat or grab a drink in McDonald's or Burger King restaurants and ask for monedas in your change. They usually have them and will give you a couple of pesos.
• Fib when asked by cashiers if you have monedas, so that you'll get some in your change.

Eat The food

I have never had cause to complain about the food in Buenos Aires: it suits me. Home-grown succulent rump or fillet steak, fresh salads, desserts with *dulce de leche* (a thick cold caramel sauce) — I've almost forgotten that I used to love curries, spicy poppadoms and black pepper with everything... it's not that you *can't* get them here, but sometimes the prices are out of my league. You guys, here on holiday, should have few complaints. Even vegetarians have options, although it has to be said that in the land of *carne*, *carne* and more *carne* (meat), you might never want to hear the word *parrilla* (grill) again. As a tango dancer I find I get hungry at all times of the day and night. I need big and late breakfasts, after-tango-class energy boosters, pre-milonga steaks, post-milonga pick-me-ups. The great news is that there is always a food-stop open in Buenos Aires, at whatever hour, and you probably won't ever have to travel too far to find it. From traditional cafés, to trendy restaurants, to the fast-food stands at the city's markets, or to cooking for yourself, here are a few of your options.

The cafés

I like the traditional cafés — and not necessarily the famous or posh ones: places like Santa Fe 1234 (open 24 hours), on Avenida Santa Fe near its corner with Libertad in Barrio Norte. In a friendly spot like that I can have a *café con leche y tres medialunas* (for details of what that is, see **Fast food**) for breakfast, a cheese omelette and three-item salad for lunch, a *licuado de banana con leche* (banana smoothie) for an afternoon lift, and a reasonably priced *bife de chorizo con papas fritas* (a rump steak with fries) for dinner; that's good enough for me. These sorts of café/restaurants tend to have a TV showing news or the footie, newspapers, waiters in traditional garb, free WiFi, and a come and go feeling that I like — I can relax with a book in the corner, as I did often in my early months here, and know that I am safe and that I can stay for as long as I want (you are never under pressure to pay up and leave fast in any Buenos Aires café or restaurant). The prices in the traditional cafés vary according to the location and history of the café, as well as where you sit: Santa Fe 1234, located on a major avenue, won't necessarily be the cheapest in town; one of my favourites when I'm being treated, the Brighton (**thenewbrightonsrl.com.ar**) at Sarmiento 645, is a traditional haven just off the calle Florida, the busiest pedestrian drag in Buenos Aires, but its historic pedigree racks up the prices — if the Brighton's too pricey for your lunch stop, try the fascinating and popular-with-local-businessmen Café Paulin a few steps away at number 635; and sitting outside in the sun, anywhere, can often be more expensive than a stool at the bar. The trendier parts of Palermo and San Telmo have a plethora of more stylish cafés to choose from, but sometimes the prices are hiked for the tourist market. In San Telmo, try Bar Británico on the corner of Defensa and Brasil; in Palermo, try Bâraka at Gurruchaga 1450 (no alcohol) for great coffee and homemade cakes.

The restaurants

The trendier (and sometimes tourist-oriented) places are more expensive than the traditional cafés, but the selection is plentiful and many have menus available in English. Areas famous for restaurants, bars and cafés are: Palermo Soho and Palermo Hollywood; Las Cañitas, particularly in and around the streets Báez and Arce where they cross Arevalo; San Telmo (start at the corner of Defensa and Estados Unidos); and Puerto Madero (the waterside, renovated-docklands district).

There are more parrilla-style restaurants than any other kind because the Argentine speciality is meat, and especially beef: a zillion different cuts, sausages, every organ imaginable... they love it grilled, or sometimes crucified and cooked around a central fire. If you are a meat eater, you will be happy, and especially so because the quality is top-notch, while the prices are good value.

Rather than recommend individual restaurants, I'll point you to the Guía Oleo (**guiaoleo.com.ar**), an excellent guide to the restaurants of Buenos Aires. In the Guía Oleo, you can find restaurants by criteria such as the *Zona* (district), *tipo de cocina* (type of cooking), with *delivery* (takeaway), WiFi, *tenedor libre* (eat as much as you want, buffet style), *Vegetariana* (vegetarian); guide prices are given.

Fast food

Empanadas (small filled pasties) are perhaps the most famous Argentine snack, available in most cafés and many milongas too. Fillings vary from the common *carne* (minced beef), *pollo* (chicken) and *jamón y queso* (ham and cheese) to more exciting options in specialist places, for example Roquefort, *choclo* or *humita* (sweetcorn and probably cheese) and *verdura* (spinach or Swiss chard). Empanadas are the cheapest snack available at just a few pesos each.

A more meaty traditional treat is a *choripán* — a grilled sausage (*chorizo*) in bread (*pan*). For a great one, head to Feria de Mataderos (see **See** later in **Part 4** for details) on a Sunday and find El Rey del Chori, a stall in the main square; if you don't fancy meat, there are plenty of other delicious options cooked up at the food stands nearby.

The truly fast-food equivalent is the *pancho* (hot dog), which is a pre-cooked sausage kept hot in boiling water... they have them the world over I think, and in my view they're ghastly everywhere.

Perhaps the most common fast lunch in cafés is the *tostado mixto* (a toasted ham and cheese sandwich). If you don't want the ham, say *sólo queso* (just cheese).

Pizza is hugely popular among Argentines, and Avenida Corrientes in the few blocks each side of the Obelisco is the biggest pizza zone — try Las Cuartetas at Corrientes 838 (Microcentro) or Guerrin at Corrientes 1368 (Centro). You can usually buy a *porción* (slice) if you can't eat a whole one: even the *chica* (small) can be enough for two.

For breakfast, afternoon tea or indeed any time around the clock, Argentines eat *medialunas* (a half-moon-shaped croissant-style speciality). Medialunas come in two varieties: *de manteca* (buttery, cake-like in texture and sweet — the best ones are light and fluffy, the worst are dry) and *de grasa* (less sweet, flakier in texture and narrower — the best ones are soft and look a bit undercooked, the worst are hard enough to break your teeth). Most cafés do a breakfast offer of *café con leche y tres medialunas* (milky coffee and three medialunas); sometimes the offer lasts all day, though medialunas are best eaten fresh.

For the foreign fast-food desperados, McDonald's and Burger King restaurants are dotted liberally all over the city. The Burger King restaurant on the corner of Florida and Corrientes is in a historic building and is a must-see for its ceilings on the first floor (go upstairs and take a look — you will be amazed, I promise).

Some options for vegetarians

In the capital city of meat, is all lost for the veggies among us? Apparently not. Vegetarian friends tell me they have survived. Italian restaurants are plentiful and offer non-meat pasta and pizza options: the *fugazza con muzzarella* (onion and mozzarella cheese pizza) is a particular favourite of mine; a wide range of vegetarian empanadas are available in some empanada-specialist restaurants; in traditional cafés, an omelette, but *sin jamón* (without ham), can be a good option for lunch or breakfast; and there are increasing numbers of good vegetarian restaurants dotted around the city. A delicious alternative in the parrilla is the grilled Provolone cheese called *provoleta*, usually with oregano, or sometimes grilled vegetables are available. Salads are always on offer and you can often request a mix of three or five different *gustos* (flavours/items).

Here are five vegetarian places spread around the city:

- Sattva (**sattva.com.ar**) at Montevideo 446, Centro
- Buenos Aires Verde (**bsasverde.com**) at Gorriti 5657, Palermo
- Artemisia (**artemisianatural.com.ar**) at Gorriti 5996, Palermo
- Naturaleza Sabia (**www.naturalezasabia.com.ar**) at Balcarce 958, San Telmo
- Arevalito (Facebook **Arevalito**) at Arévalo 1478, Palermo

Castellano you might need:

Soy vegetariano/vegetariana — I'm vegetarian.

Sin carne, por favor — without meat, please (if you're not in a vegetarian restaurant, I suggest you always say this, even if the menu item doesn't mention meat).

Eating out — meal times, credit cards and tips

Meal times in Argentina are flexible, with most traditional cafés serving everything on their menu all day, and some, all night. In the restaurants, however, dinner time is relatively late by most foreigners' standards, from around 10pm, so if you go out to eat earlier, you could find yourself facing either closed doors or the prospect of dining alone. After 10pm, in the more popular places in Palermo and Las Cañitas, there will be long wait-lists, with everyone hanging out on the street until their name is called. Reservations are not always possible — just put your name down when you arrive.

Tarjetas de crédito (credit cards) might not be taken, so check first.

A 10% tip is the custom and will be welcomed in restaurants and cafés.

Self-catering

A few major supermarkets are Dia, Coto, Jumbo, Disco and Carrefour. They are ultra-convenient for picking up everything you need in one go without having to speak any foreign languages! You might be asked to put your bag in a locker on the way in; you might have to get your fruit and vegetables weighed in the fruit and vegetable section before heading for the checkout; in the bigger places, you might find a good deli counter with a range of precooked convenience food, in case you are feeling lazy. Queues can be long, and service at the checkouts slow: I used to get stressed over the long waits, but now I know it's the same everywhere and I relax and read a book instead. You can pay with a credit card, but you may need your passport — sometimes a copy will suffice, and sometimes not.

In addition to the major supermarkets, there are *minimercados* (smaller supermarkets) everywhere. The range of individual *verdulerías* (greengrocers, where it isn't the done thing to handle the produce yourself), *panaderías* (bakers) and *carnicerías* (butchers) is staggering, though in some areas they can seem in short supply: for example, when walking certain streets in Recoleta, you may think that people have to survive on antiques, designer clothes and pristine white babygrows.

If you want Asian food, spices and imports that you didn't know existed, then head for Barrio Chino: start at the corner of Juramento and Arribeños in Belgrano (nearest Subte station, Juramento on Line D) and walk down Arribeños towards Mendoza. The Buenos Aires 'Chinatown' is relatively small, but here are several supermarkets stocking an impressive range of ingredients, including spices, vegetables, fruit and imported products.

For those living in San Telmo, El Mercado de San Telmo (see **San Telmo** in **Choosing a location**, under **Sleep**) is the best place for fresh produce, and it's so good that sometimes the thought of it makes me wish I lived in the barrio of San Telmo.

Speak Some options for learning the lingo

English isn't commonly spoken in Buenos Aires by your average man or woman in the street. When I arrived, back in 2007, neither my taxi driver nor the people running my hostel nor the folk managing the local internet café, from where I was trying to call home, spoke a word. I fast realised that if I wanted to connect with the locals, it was going to have to be in Spanish.

Do all you can to learn a bit of Castellano (the brand of Castilian Spanish spoken in Buenos Aires), or even straight Spanish. You will be able to converse so much more easily, especially with the people you dance with in the milongas. Remember that between tangos there is a break and you will find yourself standing on the dance floor facing your partner for at least fifteen seconds, while everyone chats around you: wouldn't it be nice if you could exchange a few words?

Before you come

The more Castellano or Spanish you know before you get here, the better. Perhaps you'll find a group class or a private teacher in your own country. Or perhaps you'll want to try a Do It Yourself course via books, DVDs, CDs or internet downloads. If you fancy the DIY method for learning Castellano, here are a couple of options, and in fact, a combination of the two could work out rather well.

Bueno, entonces... by **generallinguistics.com** is a quick-paced course in conversational Castellano, first released in 2009. It's as contemporary, in both material and delivery, as you could desire. Complete beginners might have to watch the classes a few times or stop and start the videos and take notes, but the material is imaginatively presented, so it wouldn't be too much of a hardship. Just for a change, this is a language course that won't send you to sleep, and it might even make you laugh. The pronunciation is perfect, and the speed of speech is realistic, so you'll get used to how the Argentines merge their words. It's a bit naughty — you'll learn the rude stuff you might require if you either end up in bed with an Argentine, or need to get angry with one. Mind you, if you're easily shockable, you mightn't like it, so beware. You can buy it on DVD or as an internet download. Watch the demos on the website before you buy, and find out if it could suit you.

Enjoy the Tango of Learning Spanish by Demian Gawianski at **www.tangospanish.com** is a book with CDs. It teaches Castellano (and explains the differences between Castellano and Spanish). Its unique selling point is that it was specifically created for tango dancers and so the entire course is set in the world of tango. Brilliant! I used it during my first weeks in Argentina, and I still use it as a reference book today. The website also offers classes both before you come, long distance via the internet, and in Buenos Aires, and now there is also a two-DVD set.

Once you're here

Here are four Buenos Aires language schools that my friends have enjoyed. They offer intensive courses taught in group classes; all cater for absolute beginners upwards (if you are not a beginner, they will usually ask you to take a test to determine your level); and all offer private classes, either as a supplement to or instead of the intensive courses. The schools vary in character, teaching methods, maximum number of students in a class and the course materials provided. There may be a minimum course length. Some offer extra-curricular cultural activities and tours, which can be good opportunities to get to know the other students; some can arrange accommodation with host families (an excellent way to practise your Castellano, but whether it would work out for tango dancers who are likely to be coming and going from milongas in the middle of the night – not sure); and some have a common room where students can relax, use the internet or have a coffee. Prices are similar across all these schools, but some charge a registration fee in addition to the course fee, and others don't, so be sure to confirm exactly what is included, and what isn't.

It's advisable (especially if you are on a short trip and your dates are fixed) to make contact in advance of your arrival in Buenos Aires to check availability for your dates.

Remember, if you decide to do one of the most intensive courses, you will be attending the school most days, so location will matter. Two of these are in the Centro, one is in Palermo and one is in San Telmo:

- Academia Buenos Aires at Hipólito Yrigoyen 571, 4th floor, in the Microcentro (**academiabuenosaires.com**)
- DWS, Daniela Wasser School, at Avenida Córdoba 4382, in Palermo (**www.danielawasser.com.ar**)
- IBL, International Bureau of Language, at Florida 165, 3rd floor, in Galería Güemes, in the Microcentro (**www.ibl.com.ar**)
- Rayuela at Chacabuco 852, 1st floor 11, in the barrio of San Telmo (**spanish-argentina.com.ar**)

123teachme.com offers independent reviews of language schools in Buenos Aires, including some of those listed above.

If you fancy trying something a bit more informal and possibly a lot more fun than formal classes, take a look at Spanglish Exchange (**spanglishexchange.com**). Their two-hour-long events are held in various bar locations around the city and give you the opportunity to practise your Spanish with locals who want to learn English. The method is that you get paired up, speak for five minutes in English then five minutes in Spanish, and then move on to a new partner. I haven't tried it myself, but it sounds like it could be a cool way to learn through practice, and to meet fellow travellers and locals at the same time.

Connect From text messaging to WiFi

You're going to get to know other tango dancers in Buenos Aires and you might need to be in easy contact with them. Making arrangements to meet at the milonga, changing the plan at the last minute, calling the night off when you've burnt the candle at both ends one too many times... you could be doing it all. What works well communications-wise in Buenos Aires? If you're planning to hook up with new friends, I think having a working mobile phone, equipped with an Argentine pay-as-you-go SIM, plus an email account that you can log on to anywhere, can solve everything.

Mobile phones

Almost all visiting tango dancers seem to stay in touch via text messaging. Calling from a mobile is relatively expensive, and not everyone will have access to a landline.

Will your phone work here? If it's triband or quadband and unblocked then it should do, and you can buy a SIM card and credit from any of the major companies: Movistar, Claro and Personal. They have small branch stores everywhere. It takes a while for the SIM activation to take place; occasionally it doesn't take place at all and you may have to go back to the shop to chase things up. You can always buy a cheap (basic low function) mobile phone here, if yours doesn't work with an Argentine SIM.

Mobile numbers are eight digits prefixed by either 15 or 11. When dialling a mobile phone from a landline, you must use 15 and not 11 as the prefix, regardless of whether the number is normally prefixed by 15 or 11.

Topping up the credit is straightforward. A reliable method is to buy a card for your network in a *Locutorio* (for details, see **Internet and WiFi**). The instructions are on the card in Castellano, but I think you can work it out. You can send a text message with the unique number from the scratch-off panel or call and, when requested to do so, enter the unique number, usually followed by a '#' (it's called the *numeral* in Castellano). Check that the card is unused and hasn't been tampered with before you leave the shop. *Carga virtual* (electronic charging) is another option in some locutorios and supermarkets.

Castellano you might need:

Quiero comprar una tarjeta SIM para mi celular — I want to buy a SIM card for my mobile phone.

Quiero comprar un crédito de veinte pesos — I want to buy credit of twenty pesos.

Compré una tarjeta SIM ayer pero no puedo comunicarme. Por favor, me puede ayudar? — I bought a SIM card yesterday, but it's not working. Please can you help me?

Quiero una tarjeta Claro/Movistar/Personal de veinte pesos — I want a Claro/Movistar/Personal card for twenty pesos.

Internet and WIFI

Locutorios are the internet cafés. They offer internet, telephone cabins (for national and international calls), printing, fax and photocopying, as well as the sale of pre-pay phone cards (mobile phone cards and international calling cards — a reliable option for the latter is the Llamada Directa (**llamadadirecta.com**) brand, and it can be used to make calls from any landline telephone). While there remains a shortage of monedas, you might be expected to pay with the correct change in a locutorio, if your total spend is small.

WiFi is available in many hostels, hotels, cafés and restaurants in Buenos Aires... even the Subte stations offer WiFi. However, do be cautious and don't flash your laptop in public when you are not actually using it. Carry it in a bag that doesn't look like a laptop case. I don't recommend you use the WiFi available in the Subte stations, but instead, choose a quiet corner of a respectable-looking café.

See What to do with your time off tango

If it's time to take a few hours off from tango (and I think both your body and mind may thank you for it if you do), well, you are spoiled for choice in Buenos Aires. Lonely Planet, Time Out and Moon, to name but three famous brands, publish dedicated guide books to the city, and offer you a fabulous selection of sightseeing possibilities. Another excellent resource is the Official Tourism Site of the City of Buenos Aires, **bue.gob.ar**, and it's available in English (click the British flag in the top right corner of the home page). Have a really good look at it before you leave home. You'll find must-see places, the higher-profile museums, and all kinds of tours, from self-guided and literary walks to guided tours of the city parks and monuments by electric bicycle. There's a lot of practical information available too, including maps. For access to some services, you are required to register.

To get a great overview of the city early in your trip, take the Buenos Aires Bus (**buenosairesbus.com**) — an open-top bus tour. The whole circuit takes around three to three and a half hours if you don't take a break, though you can hop on and off at any of the scheduled stops, and there's a good headphone commentary to put you in the know about the city. The bus gets a roof on wet or very hot days, offers fabulous photo opportunities, and is bright yellow so you can't miss it. The official start point is Diagonal Norte and Florida in the Microcentro.

Some fine options for walking tours are the private walking tour from Buenos Tours (**buenostours.com**) or a street art tour from either Buenos Aires Street Art (**buenosairesstreetart.com**) or graffitimundo (**graffitimundo.com**).

If you find the long lists of sightseeing ideas in the guide books too daunting, or don't have a clue where to start, below are five of my suggestions. They range from a city-centre trip to possibly the most stunning bookshop on the planet, to a market complete with gauchos on horseback, about an hour from the Centro by bus. So, however much time or spirit of adventure you've got, there'll be an option for you.

El Ateneo, Galerías Santa Fe and Recoleta Cemetery

Combine this with a bit of tango shoe shopping (for the ladies). First head for El Ateneo at Santa Fe 1860 in Barrio Norte (nearest Subte station is Line D, Callao). It's a bookstore with a stunning difference… go and find out what that difference is. Walk through to the rear of the store and take in the amazing view. Make sure you look up at the ceiling, and also notice where the café is. When you can drag yourself away, turn right, walk down Avenida Santa Fe, and enter the indoor shopping mall, Galerías Santa Fe, at number 1662. Walk down the passageway until it opens out, and then look up. Even some of the corridors have ceiling murals, and sometimes art exhibitions are held in the space. Yes, I know it's perhaps a small thing to show you, in comparison to attractions such as the marvellous and must-see Recoleta Cemetery (which is fairly close, so you could walk there afterwards), but I love that there are little artistic gems like this hidden throughout Buenos Aires, and I want to encourage you to look out for them. This part of Santa Fe Avenue is a busy shopping district, and it's also fairly near Comme il Faut, so you could follow this bit of low-key sightseeing with some clothes or tango shoe shopping.

Palacio Barolo

If there is a more panoramic view of the Buenos Aires skyline than from the top of this beautiful building at Avenida de Mayo 1370, in the Centro near the Congreso building, then I have not found it. You climb around one hundred metres to a glass lighthouse, which from the outside reminds me of the pinnacle of a fantasy wedding cake. This highlight comes at the end of an hour-long tour (in Spanish and English) that reveals the fascinating story of how the architecture of the Palacio Barolo was inspired by *The Divine Comedy*, Dante's epic three-part poem about heaven, hell and purgatory. If you only take one tour while you are in Buenos Aires, this has to be the one.

Do call ahead to book places on the tour (**palaciobarolotours.com.ar**), because numbers in the lighthouse are limited. The tour runs on Monday and Thursday afternoons.

Museo de Bellas Artes de La Boca, Benito Quinquela Martín

I'm assuming you will go to La Boca to see Caminito, possibly the most famous (and most touristy, other than the pedestrianised Florida and Lavalle) street in Buenos Aires, while you are here. When you do, take an hour to step off the hectic tourist trail and enter this wonderful museum (**museoquinquela.gov.ar**). Benito Quinquela Martín was a painter born in La Boca, and his large paintings of life in the port area, as well as a reconstruction of his apartment, are exhibited. You'll find a collection of rather beautiful ships' figureheads, temporary art exhibitions and outdoor sculpture terraces on the roof. Make sure you get up to the highest rooftop level (towards the waterfront) and see the view. The museum is closed on Mondays. Find it at Avenida Pedro de Mendoza 1835. Get there by radio taxi (if you can afford it, as it's a distance from the city centre) or by bus: the 64, 29 and 152 pass through the centre and down to La Boca, or it's a hop-off-and-on stop on the Buenos Aires Bus. If you want a cool lunch stop while you're down in La Boca, head for PROA (**proa.org**) just down the road at 1929 and find the café, with its own super view and tasty fresh food, on the top floor.

Calle Lanín

Calle Lanín is an intriguing street in the barrio of Barracas, where more than thirty-five homes have become canvases for exciting ceramic art. As yet, this street remains undiscovered by most tourists, because it's a fair distance from the city centre and also because Barracas isn't thought to be one of the safest districts of Buenos Aires: I think it's worth an adventurous spirit and a step off the well-trodden tourist trail. The Calle Lanín project began in the 1990s when the artist Marino Santa María (**www.marinosantamaria.com**), who lives in the street, decorated the outside of his home with ceramic mosaic work. Later money was donated to enable other home-owners to follow suit. The result is a street with a rich and vibrant soul.

I visit by bus number 12, during the afternoon on weekends, when there are usually a few people around. Catch the 12 on Avenida Santa Fe at any 12 bus stop between Fitz Roy and Riobamba; get off on Avenida

Montes de Oca in Barracas, close to the cross-street called Suárez; from Montes de Oca you have to cross under the *autopista* (motorway) 9 de Julio, and you can do it on Suárez. Alternatively you could take a radio taxi and arrange for it to wait for you or ask it to come back in thirty minutes or so, depending on how many photographs you want to take. Start at Suárez and Lanín and walk the full length of Lanín, then turn around and walk back to the corner where you started.

Feria de Mataderos

Perhaps this is my favourite Sunday out in Buenos Aires. A simple taste of the countryside in a city market — live music and folk dancing in the street, delicious takeaway food, quality crafts at reasonable prices, country people in traditional costume, gauchos racing on horseback in the quest for 'the ring' (go and discover!). The *Museo Criollo de los Corrales* (Creole Museum of Los Corrales), at Avenida de los Corrales 6436, serves up the history.

The Feria de Mataderos is in the city, but an hour from the centre by bus, in the barrio of Mataderos. It's on Sundays from 11am to early evening, from mid April through to mid December, with the horseback entertainment usually kicking off around the middle of the afternoon; during the summer break, a cut-down version of the fair is held on some Saturday evenings. If it rains heavily, it's not on. Safety-wise, it's best to stick to the market area, where there will be lots of people, rather than to wander off into deserted streets.

Always check the website **feriademataderos.com.ar** before you go, to confirm it's on and for the programme, and to find out which buses you can take there (for that, click on *Acceso*). One straightforward bus option is the 55 from any 55 bus stop on Thames (running through Palermo). Get off the 55 in Mataderos on Avenida Directorio at the corner with Lisandro de la Torre. The 55 bus back to Palermo goes from Avenida Directorio heading in the opposite direction. The Caserón Porteño Tango Map helpfully shows the barrio of Mataderos in a rectangular box at the top of the Map South.

Survive Be safe and well

Stay safe

People always ask me if Buenos Aires is safe for tourists. I have never had any problems. By day, I have travelled by taxi (radio and non radio), the Subte, bus, train, and walked vast distances. And on countless nights, I have come and gone from milongas in the early hours. From day one, I made the decision that worrying about safety would not stop me from dancing tango, at whatever hour, in whatever place. But that doesn't mean I ignore the fact that danger may exist.

While I often take a bus to a late-night milonga, I take a radio taxi home, unless *I know for sure* that the entire walk to the bus stop and the bus stop itself are in a busy, well-lit area with plenty of people around (for example, from El Beso to my bus stop on Callao – the junction of Corrientes and Callao is one of the busiest in the city, and never sleeps). Some areas are less safe than others, especially at night, and you can feel it and see it. For example, San Cristóbal, Constitución and parts of Abasto, Almagro, Monserrat, Once and San Telmo are shuttered up and feel edgier as the hours of darkness fall, and it's sensible to be especially careful. Other spots, like Palermo around Plaza Italia or the centres of Palermo Soho and Palermo Hollywood, are like Piccadilly Circus whatever the time of day or night, and people will be eating and drinking at pavement cafés until dawn; mind you, there are plenty of quieter side streets too, and it's best to stick to the main drag. I realise that I know the city and you may not, and I suggest that first-timers in Buenos Aires may prefer to take radio taxis both to and from the late-night milongas, as I did when I first arrived here. In **20 Places to Try First** in **Part 3**, I have given you directions to the nearest spot where you should be able to catch a radio taxi after each milonga. In all areas it's best to wait or walk with others rather than alone, and to try not to advertise the fact that you are tourists (by speaking English in loud voices, for example). If you feel at all uneasy, wait at the doorway of the venue until a taxi passes, or if you get really stuck, go back inside the venue and ask the host if they would mind calling one for you.

In the milonga itself, if you ever feel threatened when you are alone, although I never have, I would suggest asking the host for assistance, or listening out for another foreigner of your own sex and perhaps approaching them.

Castellano you might need:

Discúlpeme, podría conseguirme un taxi, por favor? — Excuse me, please could you call me a taxi?

The most common crimes affecting tourists seem to be: bag grabs in cafés and bars in tourist hot spots (keep your bag on your knee in front of you); taxi drivers exchanging your good $100 peso note for a forgery (use small denomination notes); cameras or mobile phones being snatched from tables in cafés (keep valuables hidden in your bag); scammers tipping fake bird shit on you and nabbing your wallet while pretending to help you (refuse any help offered in this situation, and keep your hands on your valuables instead); used phone cards being sold as new (check the scratch-off panel is intact before leaving the shop); gold chains being pulled from the wearer in touristic spots; pick-pocketing in crowds, including on the subway and buses... in other words, petty rather than very violent stuff. It is true that a few friends of mine have experienced muggings (at night, on back streets) and bag or camera snatches (in broad daylight, sometimes with the thief speeding past on a motorbike). It definitely pays to be alert, but there's no need to be paranoid.

Stay well

Make sure you've got travel insurance before you come because if you get sick or have an accident you'll be paying for private facilities here, and of course you will want to claim it all back.

If you need to see a *médico* (doctor) in Buenos Aires, your best option is to visit one of the excellent private hospitals as an outpatient. You will have to pay an outpatient fee, and show your passport. I have done this myself: I went to the Hospital Alemán (**www.hospitalaleman.com.ar**), which is fairly centrally located at two blocks from the Line D Subte station Pueyrredón, on the corner of Pueyrredón and Beruti in Barrio Norte. I went on a Sunday, was seen efficiently and treated successfully by an English-speaking doctor. There are no guarantees, but most of the doctors I have consulted in Argentina have spoken pretty good English when I've needed it. You can ask — *Usted habla inglés?* (Do you speak English?). If you need X-rays or further tests, you pay for them as you use the services. If you are given prescriptions, you can fill and pay for them at any chemist. Branches of Farmacity are easy to spot and reliable. All chemists display a green cross symbol. The bigger branches of Farmacity are open 24/7 for a 'through the window' service.

Need help?

If you go to one of the local *comisarías* (police stations) you'll probably have to speak Spanish. However, the Tourist Police Station (Corrientes 436) has English speakers, and the police in the comisarías can call on them to come and translate for you if necessary. If you are the victim of a crime and wish to report it to the police, the fastest course of action is to head to the nearest comisaría to where the crime happened. If you go to the Tourist Police Station, they will send you back there anyway to officially report the crime. I experienced this situation for myself when a friend had her handbag stolen in 2012.

The Official Tourism Site of the City of Buenos Aires is **bue.gob.ar** and it gives these details for visitors:

Tourist Police Station:
Address: Avenida Corrientes 436
Telephone: 0800 999 5000 / 4346 5748

If you phone, you should be able to speak to someone in English. It might be wise to carry these telephone numbers with you in case you need them while out. They are also given in the Tango Map Guide.

Before travelling, find out the address of your own country's embassy in Buenos Aires and register with them if they suggest it, via whatever process they recommend. Then they will know you are in Argentina, in the unlikely event that you need to call on them.

The Future of *Happy Tango*

Buenos Aires is a fast-changing city, and its tango scene is no exception. Between this and any future editions, occasional updates will be published to the book's 'Updates Blog' at **sallycatway.com/happytango** and to the book's Facebook page **facebook.com/happytango** — please 'Like' the Facebook page and visit it regularly to get the latest news.

If you'd like to share your experiences of using this second edition, please comment on the posts on the book's Facebook page or email your feedback to **happytango@pirottapress.com** where it may even help to inform future editions of the book.

Happy Tango is independently published; the paperback is available from the major online book sellers worldwide and e-versions are planned. If you enjoy ***Happy Tango***, please help me to spread word of the book by telling your tango-dancing friends about it. Thank you!

Appendix A

10 TANGO SCHOOLS

DNI Tango **dni-tango.com** Bulnes 1011 (Almagro)	Lovingly renovated townhouse studios, hosting classes in tango (levels 1 to 7) and other dance forms, from Monday to Saturday. A práctica is offered on Saturday afternoon. Famous for tango nuevo in the DNI style.
El Amague Tango Milonguero **elamague.blogspot.com.ar** Perón 1602 (Congreso)	Classes are usually held on Monday, Thursday and Friday evenings, along with occasional Friday night prácticas featuring live music. The El Amague school has had several homes over the past two years, so it's best to check the regularly updated website for the latest news and for details of the class locations, times and prices.
El Beso **elbesotangobar.com.ar** Riobamba 416 (Centro)	Classes are hosted in this world-famous milonga venue throughout the week. La Academia de Tango Milonguero **laacademiatango.com** holds evening classes on Monday, Wednesday and Friday at 8.30pm and on Sunday at 8pm and offers a práctica on Monday night after the class.
Escuela Argentina de Tango **eatango.org** (subscribe for updates) *Sede* (location) 1: Galerías Pacífico, Centro Cultural Borges, 2nd level (Microcentro) — easiest to find if you enter through the doors on Viamonte at its corner with San Martín. Sede 2: Talcahuano 1052 (Barrio Norte)	Well-known dance school based in two city-centre locations: its flagship venue is a dedicated studio space in a prestigious downtown spot, above the Galerías Pacífico shopping mall. A wide range of classes run back-to-back from 9.30am to 10pm every day, and many are taught by famous names. Great chance to try out different teachers. Call in to the reception desk at either of the school's locations to get the latest programme.
Estudio La Esquina **estudiolaesquina.blogspot.com** Sarmiento 722, 4th floor (Mi	The light and airy studio space of Vilma Vega and Fernando Galera, in a central downtown location. A variety of classes is offered from Monday to Saturday from around lunchtime (times vary by the day of the week). Call in for the current schedule.

La Escuela del Tango

escueladeltango.blogspot.com.ar

San José 364, 3rd floor, Apt A
(Monserrat)

Pleasant studio space in a lovely old building. Classes are held at specific times only, on Monday to Friday, and the regular schedule is clearly presented on the website. An Integral Training Technique for dancers is offered by the school's director, Claudia Bozzo; see **tecnicasintegradastango.blogspot.com.ar**

La Viruta

lavirutatango.com

Asociación Cultural Armenia,
Armenia 1366
(Palermo)

A cavernous basement space hosting popular classes in tango, rock and salsa, during the evenings from Tuesday to Sunday. The class schedule and the hours of the prácticas that follow the classes are published on the website.

Mariposita

mariposita.com.ar

Carlos Calvo 948/950
(San Telmo)

Antique building, beautifully renovated in a contemporary style, housing the boutique hotel and dance studios of Carolina Bonaventura. Classes run at various times from Monday to Saturday. See website for the regular schedule.

The 'Sunderland prácticas'

Facebook
Carlos y Rosa Pérez
info@carlosyrosaperez.com.ar
sunderlandclub.com.ar

Club Sunderland,
Lugones 3161, Villa Urquiza

Monday and Wednesday from 8pm. Popular with those who want to learn and practise their tango (including their walk) in the 'Villa Urquiza' style under the watchful eyes of Carlos and Rosa.

As the venue is distant from the city centre, check it's definitely on before you travel.

Tango Escuela Carlos Copello

Facebook
Tango Escuela Carlos Copello
Anchorena 575
(Abasto)

Intriguing space with a theatrical vibe, housing a small café/bar and several dance studios, where classes in tango and other dance forms are offered at various times throughout the week. Call in for the latest schedule.

Appendix B

10 TANGO SHOE STORES

Sample Tango Shoes (handwritten, left margin)

2x4alpie

2x4alpie.com

Scalabrini Ortiz 1753, Depto 3
(Palermo)
*Men's tango shoes plus ranges of
practice shoes for both sexes*

Brilliant, unique interchangeable sole
system that really does work in their
trendy tango-shoe designs for men.
High level of comfort, quality materials
and Argentine craftsmanship, and
popular with the professionals. No
longer making women's tango shoes,
though dance sneakers are available.

Alanis

Facebook
Alanis Tango Shoes

Avenida Roque Saenz Peña/Diagonal
Norte 936 (Microcentro)
Women and men

Could be the lightest women's shoe I
have ever worn, and I confess I am a fan.
Good cushioning underfoot and
gorgeous combinations of coloured and
metallic leathers. Store is handily
located just around the corner from the
cluster of shoe stores in Suipacha street.
If you're lucky, Silvia Alanis will be
there to advise when you visit.

Comme il Faut

commeilfaut.com.ar

Arenales 1239, Puerta 3 Dto M
(Recoleta)
Women only

right on Montevideo (handwritten)
ill Arenales' (handwritten)

The sexiest stilettos in Tangoland?
Ever-changing range of limited editions,
but very few shoes are on display in the
store: you have to go in with an idea of
what you want, and the assistants bring
you a selection. Loved by women (and
men!) all over the globe.

Darcos

darcosdanceshoes.com

Sarmiento 835 (Microcentro)
Men and women

The Darcos 'mega store' on Sarmiento
street is a place to browse many styles of
shoe at once and get an idea of
current prices. Lots of choice, and tango
clothes also available.

DNI

dni-tango.com

Bulnes 1011 (Almagro)
Men and women

Store is located in the DNI tango school,
so you could combine shoe shopping
with a class. Hip designs, plus comfort
and stability that can cope with an
energetic open-embrace style of tango.
Dance clothing too.

Flabella

flabella.com

Suipacha 263 (Microcentro)
Men and women

Some swear by these as a trusty basic
shoe. Store is handily located in the
cluster of six different shoe stores in
Suipacha street, so you can see and
compare other brands.

GretaFlora \n\n**gretaflora.com**\n\nAcuña de Figueroa 1612 (Palermo)\n*Men and women*	Beautiful designs for women, in an array of stunning colours, many of which bear the GretaFlora signature flower. Gorgeous and well crafted.
Neo Tango\n\n**neotangoshoes.com**\n\nSarmiento 1938 (Centro)\n*Men and women*	Wide range of designs offering something for everyone. All the available styles are laid out in the shop, so you can pick up and browse easily without pressure to buy.
Soy Porteño Missé\n\n**soyporteno.com**\n\nJuan Domingo Perón 1610, 5th floor, B (Congreso)\n*Men and women*	Very sexy shoes at the killer-heel end of the spectrum for women, as well as men's shoes. They have a strong Facebook presence where they regularly post photos of the shoes, so you can see them before you come.
Taconeando\n\nFacebook\n**Taconeando Zapatos de Tango**\n\nCórdoba 4030 (Palermo)\n*Women only*	Cool designs at a reasonable price: many have a younger vibe, and the metallic leathers are stunning. Previous visitors to Taconeando, note the new address, as the Recoleta store has closed.

If these ten don't do it for you, then you could try the group of shoe stores in the district of Abasto: Tango 8 (**tango8.com**) and Loló Gerard at 602 and 607 Anchorena street, and Artesanal de Susana Villarroel (**shoes-susanaartesanal.com**) at Jean Jaures 465. Or, in San Telmo there are several options: Vívíana Barreíero (Facebook **Vb Tangoshoes** — previously supplier to Tango Brujo, now closed) is at Independencia 389, Raquel (**raquel-shoes.com**) is at Bolívar 554 and Delié (**delieshoes.com.ar**) is at Piedras 843. In the Centro, Fabio Shoes (**fabioshoes.com.ar**) can be found at Riobamba 10, apartment 10 A.

To find other shoe designers and brands not mentioned here, keep an eye on the advertisements in the tango magazines and on the listings in the Caserón Porteño Tango Map Guide (see **The Listings** in **Part 3** for details of these sources).

Sallycat's Tango Teacher

ARIEL YANOVSKY

Thanks to Ariel, my body has the knowledge, skills and understanding of tango that free my soul to dance. He is a beautiful dancer, is a great teacher and speaks excellent English. He has become my friend.

You can see him dance with me on YouTube in the short film, *Tango Mediodía de Viernes*, shot by our mutual friend and award-winning film maker Catrin Strong in 2008.

Contact Ariel at **blacko78@hotmail.com**

The Last Word from Sallycat

THANK YOU

How can I give back the thousands of smiles and helping hands I've received since the day I first set foot in Argentina? This book continues to be my thank you. It's my wish that tango tourists have a great time in Buenos Aires, go home happy and want to return. It's my belief that if tango tourists are in the know before they come, their impact on Buenos Aires tango will be happy too: they will understand what they see, they will fit right in fast and they will ruffle fewer feathers among the local people. This book is my attempt to give the best possible experience to tourists and, by knock-on effect, to the wonderful porteños who have helped me to find joy in Argentina. The first edition of **Happy Tango** was published in 2010 and it has helped tango dancers from all over the globe to discover Happy Tango in Buenos Aires. I am delighted that the success of the book has led to this second edition. In this life, I want to be able to say that I tried. **Happy Tango** is proof that I have.

① **Usted habla inglés**
(rofoquese nu boi English)

② Discúlpeme, podría
conseguirme un taxi,
per favor
(Please, call the taxi)

③ Panaterias— boulangery

CPSIA information can be obtained at www.ICGtesting.com
Printed in the USA
LVOW05s0846271213

367048LV00004B/525/P